D1550626

# The COBBLESTONE Companion

## A Teacher's Activity Guide

### Charlene A. Forsten

Cobblestone Publishing, Inc.
20 Grove Street
Peterborough, NH 03458

For Heather and Chester...

**Picture Credits**
*A Coloring Book of the Civil War,* Bellerophon Books, 1985: Blackline Master #16; COBBLESTONE, August 1983: Blackline Master #33; COB-
BLESTONE, August 1980: Blackline Master #10; COBBLESTONE, February 1980: Blackline Master #22 (Vivian Day); COBBLESTONE, July 1982:
Blackline Master #28; COBBLESTONE, June 1982: Blackline Master #27 (Jill Shaffer); COBBLESTONE, May 1982: Blackline Master #26; COBBLESTONE,
October 1983: Blackline Master #34; Dover Publications: Blackline Masters #9 (from *The Exploration of the Colorado River and Its Canyons,*
1961) and #37; Hancock Shaker Village: Blackline Master #31; *Handbook of Early Advertising Art* by Clarence P. Hornung, Dover Publications: cover illustrations, Blackline Masters #13, #30 and #35; *Harter's Picture Archives for Collage and Illustrations* edited by J. Harter, Dover
Publications: cover illustrations; Stephen K. Kruse/COBBLESTONE, January 1980: Blackline Master #5; Stephen K. Kruse/COBBLESTONE, May
1980: Blackline Master #8; The Daily News, Longview, Washington: Blackline Master #17.

Designed by Diane Sawyer

Acknowledgments
With special thanks to Hope Pettegrew for her confidence; Carolyn Yoder for her guidance; and Debbie
Rodenhiser for her assurance.

Manufactured in the United States of America.

ISBN 0-9607638-4-8

# Contents

*Blackline Master provided for the activity

*Blackline Master provided for the activity

*Blackline Master provided for the activity

*Blackline Master provided for the activity

# Introduction

COBBLESTONE Companion is designed to supply educators with a "buffet" of activities to use in the classroom. Its intention is to embrace a variety of skills, to consider students' diversified needs, to enhance reading in the content areas, and to help you as a teacher move toward a more integrated day. Subscribers of COBBLESTONE have written not only to say how much they enjoy reading the magazine, but also to add how often they use it in their daily instruction. Out of this feedback, COBBLESTONE Companion emerged to provide teachers with an assortment of creative activities to use with each issue and to make these ideas adaptable for use beyond the magazine.

This book is set up with a table of contents, some general activities, a separate activity for each issue of COBBLESTONE, answer sheets for blackline masters (student worksheets), and finally, the blackline masters, which can be removed for copying.

We have attempted to present each activity in a simple, organized pattern. On each sheet, you will find an objective, needed materials, the procedure, follow-up ideas, and an adaptation suggestion. You will also find symbols designating curriculum areas that are enhanced by each activity. The areas are language arts, social studies, math, and art. It is important to note that the magazine issues themselves cover more curriculum areas than the activities in this companion.

COBBLESTONE Companion joins a line of many useful supplements to the magazine. One of these is the COBBLESTONE cumulative index, which in itself is a companion to the magazine and this teacher's guide.

Ms. Joanne Roose of Harper Woods, Michigan, has written that COBBLESTONE "helps to make history come alive." We hope this guide will add excitement to this living history and become a true "companion" to teachers.

# Explanation of Symbols

Throughout the manual, specific symbols are used to indicate which areas of the curriculum are enhanced by the activities. These symbols represent the following:

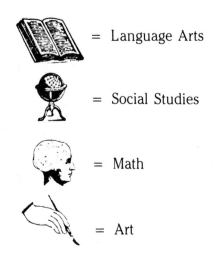

= Language Arts

= Social Studies

= Math

= Art

# Using COBBLESTONE to Help Integrate Your Reading Approach

**Objective:**    We will show you how to use COBBLESTONE as an integrated reading approach in the upper elementary grades.

**Materials:**    Issues of COBBLESTONE. (The July 1984 issue of COBBLESTONE and Blackline Master #1 will be used as models to help show you how to develop a hierarchy of comprehension questions for students to answer.)

**Procedure:**    A concern of some elementary teachers is that there seems to be a steady increase in the number of isolated subjects that must be taught. Wherever possible, curriculum integration could help alleviate this problem.

Using COBBLESTONE as a reading approach would not only integrate social studies, reading, and other language arts skills, but it would also help develop a student's ability to read in the content areas.

Here are some features and suggestions on how COBBLESTONE could be used in or as a reading approach:

- Each issue has activities on vocabulary enrichment such as word searches, scrambles, and crossword puzzles. "Word Lore" is a mini-glossary of terms used in an issue and frequently appears in the magazine. You could also make a list of vocabulary or spelling words from each issue to use in your language arts program.

- Other regular features include the following:

  - "Dear Ebenezer" (letters to the editor);
  - "Ebenezer's Bulletin Board" (a letter from the editor encouraging students to write about a future topic);
  - "Elsewhere" (briefs on what else was happening in the world at the time of the issue's theme);
  - "True or False?" (a quiz on the issue);
  - "Digging Deeper" (a bibliography suggesting books to read, places to visit, and films to rent);
  - "From the Archives" (a section suggesting other issues with related themes);
  - "Cracker's Capers" (a regular comic strip).

• Issues frequently have maps, time lines, poems, stories (fiction and nonfiction), activities, projects, contests, recipes, songs, and games.

• Several teachers have written to say that they use COBBLESTONE for student research and writing projects.

• The following issues offer plays:

> January 1980, *Shoot in the New Year—A Mummer's Play for the New World*;
> February 1980, *Free Wheeling*;
> March 1980, *No Turning Back—A Play for Radio*;
> May 1980, *If There Had Been Television in 1869*;
> November 1980, *Family Picnic*;
> September 1983, *Close Call on Nantucket*.

• Many educators use *Bloom's Taxonomy of Educational Objectives* to help develop students' comprehension skills. It has been used in this activity to write a hierarchy of questions to check the students' reading comprehension. (Blackline Master #1 has questions that demonstrate these levels in relation to the July 1984 issue. You can simply change the information in each question to adapt it to whichever issue or reading material you are using.)

# The ABCs of COBBLESTONE

**Objective:**  The students will write their own alphabet book using people and events featured in various issues of the magazine.

**Materials:**  Issues of COBBLESTONE, paper (preferably tagboard), and coloring tools.

**Procedure:**  Explain to the class that they will be writing and illustrating their own alphabet book based on people and events featured in COBBLESTONE.

Assign a letter of the alphabet to each student. (If you have more than twenty-six students, have some work as partners. If you have fewer than twenty-six, ask for volunteers to do more than one page, then give extra credit.)

Once students have their letters, allow them time to choose a person or event beginning with that letter from any issue of COBBLESTONE.

Have students design a rough draft of their pages, each of which should include the letter, the name of the chosen person or event, and a brief description of the topic.

Once you have approved the draft, have students make the final copy of their pages.

Put all the pages together, in order, and bind the book. The class might want to choose someone to create a cover, or they might all wish to contribute to a collage cover design.

**Follow-up:**  The students could dedicate and present the book to a particular person. They also could donate it to their school or local library.

**Adaptation:**  The activity could be an individual or class project, adaptable to many academic themes.

# Twenty Questions*

**Objective:**    The students will use the format of the game *Twenty Questions* to identify people featured in the magazine.

**Materials:**    Issues of COBBLESTONE, Blackline Master #2 (Notable Person Reference List).

**Procedure:**    Explain that in the game, one student is assigned to be the leader and is questioned by the rest of the class. Prior to starting the game, the leader should choose and learn about a person featured in any issue of COBBLESTONE. The notable person should be one with whom the class is familiar. (The leader could use the Notable Person Reference List as a guide.)

The game is played with the leader in front of the class. The other students each ask one question, which the leader can answer with only a yes or no response.

Advise the students to listen carefully to all questions and responses.

A student may use his or her question to guess the identity of the notable person. If the student is correct, the game ends. If the student is incorrect, it is the next person's turn to question, and the game continues.

The game is over either when a student guesses the notable person or when classmembers have each asked a question and have not been able to identify the mystery person. Should no one guess the answer, the leader may give hints until someone identifies the person.

**Follow-up:**    The leader could give an oral biographical sketch of the notable person.

**Adaptation:**    This game helps improve listening and logical-thinking skills. You could also use categories from other academic topics as the object of this game.

---

* You might wish to title your version of the game according to the number of students who will be asking questions.

# COBBLESTONE Trivia

**Objective:**     The students will play a game that uses information from issues of the magazine.

**Materials:**     Issues of COBBLESTONE, Blackline Master #3.

**Procedure:**     If possible, prior to the game, copy the Blackline Master sections. Cut them out and paste them on tagboard, then laminate or cover them with contact paper. Blank sections have been provided should you wish to add your own trivia "answers."

Explain to students that they will be playing a game of trivia in which they will be given answers instead of questions.

On each trivia card is an answer, along with the magazine issue and page number where it can be found.

Divide the class into two teams. (Two or more students can also play in a small group.)

Have the issues of COBBLESTONE readily available.

Shuffle the trivia cards.

One student from each team draws a card at the same time. Each locates his or her designated issue of COBBLESTONE, then looks for the card's answer on the given page number. Once the answer is found, the student must state a question that would be appropriate for the answer.

The first student to give a question that fits the answer wins a point for his or her team.

The team with the most points at the end of the class period wins.

**Follow-up:**     Students might wish to learn more about some of the terms used in the game.

Students might also wish to add more trivia answers to the game.

**Adaptation:**     Students could make up their own trivia questions related to academic topics being studied at the time.

# Bookmarks

**Objective:**     The students will make bookmarks for any book whose theme also appeared in an issue of COBBLESTONE.

**Materials:**     Paper (preferably tagboard), scissors, rulers, coloring tools.

**Procedure:**     Explain to students that after they have read any book whose theme also appears in an issue of COBBLESTONE, they will make a bookmark for the book.

Have students follow these steps:

- Cut tagboard into a strip that measures six inches by two inches.

- Print the title and author of the book on the strip.

- Color an illustration on the bookmark.

- Write their name and the date on it.

**Follow-up:**     For long-term use, the bookmarks could be laminated or covered with contact paper.

The bookmarks could remain in the books for future readers to use.

A bulletin board could display the students' bookmarks.

**Adaptation:**     Students could design bookmarks for their various textbooks.

# Notable Person Reception

**Objective:** The students will each choose and research a notable person from an issue of COBBLESTONE. They will then plan a reception to which they will come dressed as and speaking like their historical figures.

**Materials:** Issues of COBBLESTONE, Blackline Masters #2 and #4 (Notable Person Reference List and Notable Person Activity: Research Sheet), costumes and props, refreshments.

**Procedure:** This activity requires long-term planning and is an excellent vehicle for parent involvement.

Explain that the class will be holding a reception for notable historical figures featured in issues of COBBLESTONE and that they will take on the roles of these people.

Make the Notable Person Reference List available to the class and give each student a copy of the Notable Person Activity: Research Sheet.

Time Line:

- Three weeks prior to the reception—Students choose a notable person they wish to represent and begin their research.

- Two weeks prior to the reception—Students share their research, costume ideas, and what they intend to include in their character roles. Students also write invitations to parents, and reception refreshments are planned.

- One week prior to the reception—Students complete final preparations for their roles. The physical setup of the reception is planned.

- Day of the reception—Students come to the reception in costume and sign a guest book in their characters' names. The students then give a one-minute oral presentation about themselves. They might make note of things that appear strange or peculiar to them if they are figures from the past.

**Follow-up:** The class could discuss which characters were portrayed best and why.

**Adaptation:** This activity could also be done with book characters, fact or fiction.

# Then & Now: Comparing Maps of the Same Area

**Objective:** The students will examine two maps of Philadelphia from different time periods and answer questions comparing the past and present.

**Materials:** January 1980 issue of COBBLESTONE, Blackline Master #5, pencils.

**Procedure:** Discuss with students how different parts of their town or city have changed with time.

Have them give specific examples of these changes.

Tell students they are going to examine two maps of Philadelphia—one made in 1682, and the other made recently.

Give each student a copy of Blackline Master #5 and have each answer the questions comparing the two maps.

**Follow-up:** Correct the maps and answer any questions students might have.

Have students make up their own questions, which they will ask their classmates orally.

Ask students if any of them have been to Philadelphia. Could they describe any area shown on the map?

**Adaptation:** Locate maps from different time periods comparing the past and present of the students' town or city.

Students could interview residents about changes they have seen over the years.

# Applying
# for a Patent

**Objective:**       The students will design their own inventions, then fill out a mock patent application form.

**Materials:**       February 1980 issue of COBBLESTONE, Blackline Master #6, pencils, coloring tools.

**Procedure:**       After reading through the above issue, discuss inventions that have affected the students' school and leisure lives.

Discuss how a person might become motivated to invent something. Ask students about particular problems or tasks that might be made easier by an invention.

Explain that all the students are going to invent something that will help solve a problem, make a task easier, or improve something that already exists.

Add that once an inventor has designed something for which he or she wants full credit, a patent must be obtained. A patent is a legal document that gives the inventor exclusive rights to his or her invention.

Have students make a rough draft of both the design and description of their inventions. Then give them Blackline Master #6 and ask them to fill out the patent application form.

**Follow-up:**       Have students describe their inventions orally to the class.

If possible, students might wish to make models of their inventions.

**Adaptation:**      Students could design tools that would help them with academic topics that cause them difficulties.

Students could research inventions they think brought about great changes in the way people live.

# Writing a
# Newspaper Story

**Objective:** The students will each write an eyewitness account of the Boston Massacre for a fictitious newspaper.

**Materials:** March 1980 issue of COBBLESTONE, Blackline Master #7, pencils, coloring tools.

**Procedure:** Ask students what it means to be an eyewitness to an event.

Discuss what would be important to remember to give an accurate report of what happened. Emphasize both the meaning and the importance of being objective.

After reading through the above issue, tell students to pretend they are eyewitnesses to the Boston Massacre and must write an account of the incident for the local newspaper. (It might be advisable to read a few current news articles to the class. If possible, read articles from different newspapers that are reporting on the same event, then ask students to note similarities and differences in the accounts.)

Give each student a copy of Blackline Master #7 and review these directions.

- Have students print their names on the line above *"Boston Star Staff."*
- Tell them to write their eyewitness accounts on the lines provided on the sheet.
- Have them draw a picture of what happened in the provided space.

**Follow-up:** Discuss how eyewitness accounts can vary. (Use the two accounts in the above issue of COBBLESTONE to stress this.) Ask students if they can give reasons why this might happen.

Discuss why it can be difficult to remember details in emergency situations.

Ask students why it is important to be accurate when reporting a news event. Discuss how people or events might be affected if inaccurate information were presented.

**Adaptation:** A group of students could act out a particular incident in front of the class. Have each student write an account of what he or she saw. Then compare the accounts to see how they differ.

# Writing a Position Paper

**Objective:** The students will each write a paper taking a position on Audubon's killing animals to study and draw them.

**Materials:** April 1980 issue of Cobblestone, paper, pencils.

**Procedure:** Either read aloud to the students or have them read "Joseph Mason's Journal" in the above issue of Cobblestone.

Discuss what it means to take a position on a particular matter. Ask students what can cause people to take specific positions. (For example, a mother who lost a child at the hands of a drunk driver would probably take a very strong position on the issue of drinking and driving.)

Have students give examples of some of their strong positions on issues. Ask them if they can give reasons for their opinions.

Explain that they will now take a position on Audubon's killing animals to study and draw them.

Stress the importance of obtaining and considering all relevant information prior to taking a position on any matter.

Have them think out their positions, then write them in paragraph form. Tell them to give specific information supporting their positions.

**Follow-up:** The students could read their papers orally to the class. Classmembers could then constructively question the reader on his or her position.

**Adaptation:** Students could take positions on a variety of current events or contemporary issues and present their opinions either orally or in writing.

# Map Interpretation

**Objective:**   The students will answer questions about the route of the Transcontinental Railway.

**Materials:**   May 1980 issue of COBBLESTONE, Blackline Master #8, pencils.

**Procedure:**   Discuss how the Transcontinental Railway was built. Ask students what they think might have been the greatest difficulties in its construction.

Explain that they are going to use a map to learn more information about the route of the Transcontinental Railway.

Give each of them a copy of Blackline Master #8 and review the directions.

They are to answer questions by using information given on the map. A few questions ask students to compute mileage, using the scale of miles. You might allow students to use string to measure the windy route and compare the length of string necessary to cover the route between two points against the scale of miles.

**Follow-up:**   Ask students if they had lived during the time when the Transcontinental Railway was being built, would they have wanted to be involved with the project in some way.

**Adaptation:**   The students could compare two different routes to one location by computing the mileage for each route, then discussing the advantages and disadvantages of each.

# Sequencing a Story

**Objective:**     The students will take events that are out of order and put them in the correct sequence.

**Materials:**     June 1980 issue of COBBLESTONE, Blackline Master #9, pencils.

**Procedure:**     Either read aloud to the students or have them read "In Search of a River's End" in the above issue of COBBLESTONE.

Discuss what it means to do or say things in sequence. Ask them why completing certain tasks or understanding stories requires correct sequence. Ask them to give examples of what can happen when things are done out of sequence (example: following a recipe or building a house).

Give each student a copy of Blackline Master #9 and review the directions. Tell them to re-create the mental pictures they had as they were listening to or reading the story. This should help them remember the order of events.

**Follow-up:**     Correct the papers and ask students which events were most difficult to put in sequence. Ask them if they can identify why they might have had difficulties.

Discuss the type of person who would go on this type of expedition. Ask what would be the greatest hazard for each of them if they had gone.

Ask if parts of this story could be called "cliffhangers". Ask what dual meaning would go with this word in relation to this particular story.

**Adaptation:**     Putting events in correct sequence is a skill that could be applied to many academic topics.

# Gallery of Games

**Objective:** The students will create their own games, give a demonstration, then make them available for use.

**Materials:** July 1980 issue of COBBLESTONE, other materials determined by the individual student's game design.

**Procedure:** Have students discuss their favorite games. Ask them what makes a "good" game.

Ask students what would be important when designing a game. List their responses on the board.

Tell students that they will each be designing a game. It could have to do with a book, a specific topic in an academic subject area, or a general idea.

Have them make a rough copy of their designs and directions of how to play their games.

Have them construct the final product and write a set of specific directions to go with the game.

Designate a day to display the "Gallery of Games." Have students demonstrate how their games are played.

Put the games on a shelf where they will be available for use.

**Follow-up:** Ask students if games can help them learn about different topics. Have them list ways games can help improve their skills.

**Adaptation:** Students could design games that help them with a subject area that needs reinforcement (example: math facts).

Students could design games for younger students to enhance skills at the lower levels.

# Explaining How to Do Something

**Objective:**   The students will read the article "Panning for Gold," then write how it is done in their own words.

**Materials:**   August 1980 issue of COBBLESTONE, Blackline Master #10, pencils.

**Procedure:**   Have students read the article "Panning for Gold" in the above issue of COBBLESTONE. Prior to the reading, ask them to pay close attention to the steps in panning for gold.

Ask students to give examples of procedures that require step-by-step explanations. Discuss what can happen if directions are not clear.

Have students think through how they would explain the procedure of panning for gold to someone. If they are not sure, suggest they read the article again.

Give each student a copy of Blackline Master #10 and review the directions.

**Follow-up:**   Ask students what else could be done to help explain how to do something (example: how to draw a diagram).

Ask students whether they learn how to do something better by listening to an explanation, reading how to do it, or watching it be done. Some may say a combination of these is helpful. Some may find the way they learn how to do something depends on the activity itself, along with factors such as how they feel and how great their interest is.

**Adaptation:**   Students could practice this skill by giving an oral or written explanation of various academic topics that involve a step-by-step procedure.

# Writing a Biographical Sketch

**Objective:** The students will write a short biographical sketch about one person featured in this issue.

**Materials:** September 1980 issue of COBBLESTONE, pencils, paper.

**Procedure:** Discuss the meanings of the words "biography" and "autobiography."

Ask a few students if they could give short biographical accounts of a brother or sister, covering only important events in their lives.

Ask a few students to give short autobiographies, including only important events in their lives.

Discuss with students what is important in a short biography and list their responses on the board.

Ask students what they think a biographical sketch might be. Explain that there is not a lot of detail, and only important points are given.

After students have read through the issue, ask them to choose a person featured in one of the articles about whom they will write a biographical sketch.

Have them list important events in the person's life before they begin writing. Once they are satisfied with their list and are sure the events are in the correct order, have them write a short biographical sketch in paragraph form.

**Follow-up:** Ask students if choosing which information is important can be difficult. Discuss ways to decide on priorities.

Have students share their biographical sketches orally with the class. Ask the class to decide whether the students chose important events to put in their biographies.

**Adaptation:** Students could write biographical accounts of notable people in fields such as art, science, math, and music.

# Simulation:
# The Election of a President

**Objective:**  The students will go through a simulated presidential election.

**Materials:**  October 1980 issue of COBBLESTONE, Blackline Master #11, pencils.

**Procedure:**  This is a brief simulation calling for students to figure out the number of electoral votes that go to each candidate, thus determining the winner of an election.

Discuss how the Democrats and Republicans make up our two major political parties. Use a recent election to talk about how our political party system works.

Explain to students that they are to pretend it is the day after the election. In this simulation, fictitious names are used for both the political parties and the candidates.

Read aloud "How We Choose Our President" in the October 1980 issue of COBBLESTONE. This article is the story of a simulation that explains how the electoral college works.

Tell students you are going to give them a sheet that lists the percentage of votes each candidate received from each state. Be sure students understand that all the state's electoral votes go to whichever candidate received more than 50 percent of the vote. Explain that 51 percent or more indicates a majority.

Give each student a copy of Blackline Master #11 and the following directions:

- Put your name and date on the paper.

- Look at the chart "Presidential Election Returns." It gives the percentage of votes each candidate received.

- Now look at the "Electoral College Tally." You will find all the states and their number of electoral votes on it. You will also find a column for each presidential candidate.

- Doing one state at a time, first look at the percentage of votes each candidate received. Decide who won the majority of votes. Then go to the "Electoral College Tally" and put the number of that state's electoral votes in the column of the winning candidate. Do this for each state.

- When you have tallied all the states, add each column. The candidate receiving 270 or more votes is the winner of the presidential election.

- Circle the name of the president-elect at the top of the column.

**Follow-up:** Discuss techniques candidates use to get votes and the influence of the media on an election.

**Adaptation:** Simulations could help students understand a variety of government processes.

# Drawing a Family Tree

**Objective:**   Each student will research his or her family genealogy, then make a family tree.

**Materials:**   November 1980 issue of COBBLESTONE, Blackline Master #12, pencils.

**Procedure:**   This is basically a home project that involves students working with parents.

Discuss the meaning of the word "genealogy." Ask students why it is important and interesting to learn about their ancestors.

Explain what a family tree is. Give each student a copy of Blackline Master #12 and ask each how a family keeps branching out.

Review the directions with them. Give them ample time to take the sheets home and complete them. Some students might wish to trace more of their family trees on the back of the sheet.

When the students have completed their family trees, ask them to share the most interesting new fact they learned.

Ask how many had parents who were born in a foreign country. How many had grandparents born in a foreign country?

Discuss any problems they had in completing their trees.

**Follow-up:**   Make a bulletin board showing the family trees.

Have students share their family trees orally with the rest of the class.

**Adaptation:**   Many students have pets. They could show their pet's genealogy.

Students could research the genealogy of a favorite historical figure.

# Identifying Reasons for Moving West

**Objective:**     The students will identify reasons why people moved west.

**Materials:**     December 1980 issue of COBBLESTONE, Blackline Master #13, pencils.

**Procedure:**     After students have read through the issue, discuss the contrast of life-styles between Virginia and Nebraska.

Ask students why they think someone would leave the comforts of the East to move to the West.

Ask students if they had lived in Willa Cather's time, what feature about life in Nebraska would have required the greatest adjustment.

Give each student a copy of Blackline Master #13 and review the directions.

**Follow-up:**     Discuss reasons why people move today. Are any reasons the same as those in the 1800s?

Discuss whether students feel Willa Cather's accomplishments were unique for a woman during that time.

**Adaptation:**     Students could discuss why they think other movements occurred, such as the movement into outer space.

# In Search of Connecticut

**Objective:**     The students will answer questions on Connecticut history, then find the one-word answers in a word search.

**Materials:**     January 1981 issue of COBBLESTONE, Blackline Master #14, pencils.

**Procedure:**     This activity could be set up as a learning center where students read the above issue, then complete the activity. It could also be a large group lesson.

After students have read the issue, discuss various points about Connecticut's history. Ask students what they enjoyed most and what they might like to learn more about.

If done in a large group, give each student a copy of Blackline Master #14 and review the directions.

**Follow-up:**     Suggest students read the Newberry Award book *The Witch of Blackbird Pond* by Elizabeth Speare.

Have students complete further research on people or events that were of interest to them.

Have students make up their own word searches, using different words from Connecticut history. They could then trade papers with other students.

**Adaptation:**     Students enjoy making their own word searches. Give each student a blank sheet of graph paper and have them list a series of words related to a specific topic. Then have them put the letters in mixed fashion in the squares on the graph paper and give their word search to another student to solve.

# Filling in a Time Line

**Objective:** The students will fill in events concerning slavery next to specific dates on a time line.

**Materials:** February 1981 issue of COBBLESTONE, Blackline Master #15, pencils, scissors, paste or glue.

**Procedure:** The slaves using the Underground Railroad to go north followed the Big Dipper, which they called the "Drinking Gourd." It led them to freedom.

Read aloud to the students "Follow the Drinking Gourd" in the above issue of COBBLESTONE. It will help them understand the significance of the constellation in helping slaves escape to the North.

Give each student a copy of Blackline Master #15 and review the directions.

Explain that this is an unusual time line and that they must cut out the slavery-related events and paste them next to the star with their corresponding dates.

**Follow-up:** Discuss slavery with the students. Ask students why they think it began and why it was accepted by so many people.

Ask the students if the term "Underground Railroad" was appropriate.

Ask students to explain the Emancipation Proclamation.

**Adaptation:** Students could fill in time lines referring to any academic topic that shows continuation over a period of time.

# Spanish Heritage Mobile

**Objective:**   The students will make mobiles showing things we have today because of our Spanish heritage.

**Materials:**   March 1981 issue of COBBLESTONE, clothes hangers, string or fish line, construction paper, magazines, scissors, paste, coloring tools.

**Procedure:**   After reading through this issue of COBBLESTONE, ask students to name things that the Spanish brought to America and that we still have today. Examples are wheat, lettuce, olives, cucumber pickles, Spanish onions, beef and dairy cattle, horses, mules, donkeys, chickens, different breeds of domestic sheep, goats, pigs, and even house cats.

List these on the board. Ask students to give examples of foods or products that come from the above sources. (They could name hamburgers, bread, leather goods, and so on.)

Explain that they will each make a mobile showing the foods or products we use today because of our Spanish heritage.

Have students think over which foods or products they want to show on their mobiles.

Have them choose five examples. They should either draw the example or cut out pictures to paste on construction paper. When these are ready, have them assemble the mobile.

Students should take a sheet of construction paper and fold it over so it hangs on the horizontal wire of the clothes hanger. On this paper, they should print "Our Spanish Heritage."

Students should then hang their pictures at varying lengths from the title paper. (They might want to cover both sides of their mobile pieces to make their ideas visible at all angles.)

**Follow-up:**   Students could explain their mobiles, then hang them in the room.

**Adaptation:**   Students can make mobiles to enhance a variety of academic topics.

# Civil War Uniforms

**Objective:** The students will follow directions to color uniforms of Confederate and Union soldiers.

**Materials:** April 1981 issue of COBBLESTONE, Blackline Master #16, coloring tools.

**Procedure:** Discuss the slavery issue and how it divided the North and the South. Ask students why they feel the North and the South differed so much.

Discuss how the tension gradually led to war. Have students name the two armies.

Give each student a copy of Blackline Master #16 and review the directions.

(Once colored, the pictures could be pasted on tagboard to make stand-up figures.)

**Follow-up:** Have students share facts of which they were unaware prior to reading this issue on the Civil War.

Discuss how our Civil War sometimes involved relatives fighting against each other, depending on whether they supported the North or the South.

**Adaptation:** When uniforms are related to a topic students are studying, they can be researched, illustrated, and colored.

# Using a Map to Draw Conclusions

**Objective:**     The students will use a map to draw conclusions about the eruption of Mount St. Helens.

**Materials:**     May 1981 issue of COBBLESTONE, Blackline Master #17, pencils.

**Procedure:**     After reading through the issue, discuss what students remember about the eruption of Mount St. Helens.

Have them share details they found interesting from the above issue.

Ask students whether they can explain factors that lead to a volcanic eruption. Then have them list effects once a volcano has erupted.

Give each student a copy of Blackline Master #17 and explain what it means to draw conclusions. Tell them they are to make the best possible judgment or give the best possible answer based on the information they are given.

Have students complete the questions on the map.

**Follow-up:**     Suggest students read the Newberry Award book *Twenty-One Balloons* by William Pene DuBois.

Have students research other volcanoes and give oral presentations to the class.

**Adaptation:**     Give students a map and ask them questions from which they must draw conclusions orally. This allows for immediate feedback and can help develop logical-thinking skills.

# A Search-and-Find Mission

**Objective:**     The students will research and find answers to questions about America's lighthouses.

**Materials:**     June 1981 issue of COBBLESTONE, Blackline Master #18, pencils.

**Procedure:**     This activity would make an excellent learning center at which students could work in their free time. Besides the above issue, other books and magazines that include information on lighthouses could be set out for use.

Ask students if any of them have been to a lighthouse. Ask about things such as the location and condition.

Tell students they are going to find answers to questions about lighthouses. Instead of beacons, they will use their heads to search and find answers to specific questions.

Have students use Blackline Master #18 and the above issue of COBBLESTONE to complete the activity.

**Follow-up:**     Discuss what it would be like to be a lighthouse keeper. Then discuss the disappearance of people as keepers and the switch to automation. Ask students if any of them would consider such a job.

A student might want to make a model of one of the lighthouses.

**Adaptation:**     Learning centers on specific themes could be set up for students to do research projects in their free time.

# Applying to Go to the Moon

**Objective:** The students will give reasons why they wish to be civilian passengers to the moon.

**Materials:** July 1981 issue of COBBLESTONE, Blackline Master #19, pencils.

**Procedure:** Discuss with students how science fiction is frequently realized in the future. Ask students if they can give examples of real things or situations that were considered to be science fiction in the past.

After reading through the above issue, discuss the history of the space program and have students note what has happened between the first step into space and where we are today.

Tell the students they are to pretend that NASA has decided to accept applications from students who wish to travel to the moon.

Have them think over their reasons why NASA should choose them to be among the first students on the moon.

Give each student a copy of Blackline Master #19 and review the directions for filling out the application.

**Follow-up:** Form a committee of students to read the applications and recommend candidates for the moon trip.

**Adaptation:** Being able to fill out a form is a skill students must have. Filling out various types of forms in school helps give students the practice they need.

# The Indian and the Buffalo

**Objective:** The students will each complete a picture showing how Indians used different parts of the buffalo in their daily lives.

**Materials:** August 1981 issue of COBBLESTONE, Blackline Master #20, reference books on Indians and buffalo, pencils, coloring tools.

**Procedure:** Either read aloud to the students or have them read the article "The Indian and the Buffalo" in the above issue of COBBLESTONE.

Discuss how Indians killed only the number of buffalo they needed and how they used all parts of the animal for food, clothing, shelter, and tools.

Ask students to give examples of the ways the buffalo was used. (Example: The Indians used buffalo skins to make their clothing and homes.) On the board, list the parts of the buffalo, then the ways Indians used each part in their everyday lives.

Give each student a copy of Blackline Master #20 and review the directions. The students will each draw a picture showing at least three things Indians made from buffalo parts.

**Follow-up:** Discuss how the arrival of whites changed the relationship between the Indian and the buffalo.

Ask if any students have seen a buffalo. Ask if it was in a zoo or in the wild. Discuss how an animal can become extinct and what can be done to prevent it.

Have students discuss or illustrate the use of the buffalo as an American symbol. Do the same with other American symbols.

**Adaptation:** Having students draw pictures to demonstrate recall and comprehension is a good alternative method to use.

# Using a Chart

**Objective:**     The students will use a chart to answer questions about inventions from the Industrial Revolution.

**Materials:**     September 1981 issue of COBBLESTONE, Blackline Master #21, pencils.

**Procedure:**     Discuss the different meanings of revolution. Ask students to describe the Industrial Revolution. Have them give specific examples of changes it caused.

Ask students what the world would be like if we did not have innovative people inventing new products and improving existing ones.

Give each student a copy of Blackline Master #21 and review the directions.

**Follow-up:**     Ask students to make a list of products they use in their homes that require electricity.

Ask students which appliance they miss most when there is a blackout.

Discuss with students how their lives might be different if they lived without electricity.

**Adaptation:**     Students could use the chart as a guide to complete a research project on inventions.

# Discovering a
# Coded Message

**Objective:**   The students will use a key for Morse code to discover a message.

**Materials:**   October 1981 issue of COBBLESTONE, Blackline Master #22, pencils.

**Procedure:**   Ask students what a code is. Have someone look it up in the dictionary if no one is sure of the meaning.

Have students give examples of types of codes.

After reading through the above issue, discuss how Samuel Morse's code helped improve communications.

Ask how it affected the Pony Express.

Give each student a copy of Blackline Master #22 and review the directions.

**Follow-up:**   Students could construct their own telegraph and receiver (see the February 1980 issue of COBBLESTONE) and practice sending their own coded messages.

**Adaptation:**   Students could design their own codes, then have other students decipher the messages.

# What Does Not Belong?

**Objective:** The students will be able to demonstrate their knowledge of what items would not belong in a nineteenth-century classroom.

**Materials:** November 1981 issue of COBBLESTONE, Blackline Master #23, pencils, coloring tools.

**Procedure:** Discuss what a classroom in the 1800s might have looked like. (Have them use the above issue as a guide.)

Have students give examples of objects that would have been in a classroom during that time period. List them on the board.

Give each student a copy of Blackline Master #23 and review the directions.

Tell students they can use any resources to help them complete the activity.

**Follow-up:** Discuss which objects in today's classroom would not have existed in the 1800s. Ask which objects existed in the classroom of the past, but are much different today. Have students examine objects in the room and predict how they might be different in the future.

**Adaptation:** This activity could be adapted to other topics that can be compared through time. This helps students develop a sense of change and growth.

# Creating a Mural

**Objective:**      The students will complete a mural illustrating the route of the Oregon Trail.

**Materials:**      December 1981 issue of COBBLESTONE, butcher paper, coloring tools.

**Procedure:**      Discuss what a mural is. Ask students what features make a good mural, including size, clarity of lettering, and color.

After reading through the above issue, explain to students that they will be making a mural that illustrates the route of the Oregon Trail.

Get a large sheet of butcher paper and hang it on a bulletin board or wall.

Using the map on pages 24 and 25 in the above issue, have students draw a skeleton of the map and route on the butcher paper.

Have students research what a traveler along the Oregon Trail might have seen or experienced. Assign different places or physical features to students and have them illustrate these on the mural.

The mural could show Conestoga wagons moving along the trail at different points on the route.

**Follow-up:**      Students could pretend they were travelers on the Oregon Trail and write journal entries describing a day enroute.

Students could make dioramas (a three-dimensional miniature scene with painted figures and background) on this subject.

Students could make a model of the Conestoga wagon.

**Adaptation:**      A mural could also be used to show a story's sequence or a time line.

# Using the Prefix "Sub"

**Objective:**  The students will be given words that begin with the prefix "sub" and will match them with their appropriate meanings.

**Materials:**  January 1982 issue of COBBLESTONE, Blackline Master #24, pencils, dictionary.

**Procedure:**  Discuss the meaning of the word "submarine." Divide it into syllables. Have students identify the prefix.

Ask a student to take a dictionary and look up the definitions of the prefix "sub." Write them on the board and ask if anyone can give examples of words using the different meanings.

Give each student a copy of Blackline Master #24 and review the directions. Tell them they can use a dictionary if they are unsure of any words or definitions.

When students are finished, correct the papers together to be sure students have a clear understanding of the words.

**Follow-up:**  Students could write sentences using the words from the activity.

This issue of COBBLESTONE has several interesting articles on the history of submarines, as well as how they work. Students might wish to complete further research on this topic.

**Adaptation:**  Other word-study activities could be prepared to help students learn the meanings of prefixes and how they affect words.

# Comparing Lifestyles: Using a Diary

**Objective:** The students will each write a diary entry for one day, then compare it to one in the issue on Old Sturbridge Village.

**Materials:** February 1982 issue of COBBLESTONE, paper, pencils.

**Procedure:** Ask students what types of things a historian might use to study the way people lived in the past. List their ideas on the board. If a personal diary or journal is not mentioned, add it to the list.

Discuss how a journal or a diary can help us learn about the past.

The journal activity follows three steps:

1. Have students write one-day journal entries describing a typical Saturday. When they have finished their journals, ask them to read them aloud. Then discuss whether these journals would be representative of typical Saturdays in the lives of today's youth. If a historian were to find them one hundred years from now, would the journals provide an accurate picture of today's youth?

2. Read the article "Farming Was Family Work" from the February 1982 issue of COBBLESTONE, followed by "Sarah Emery's Diary."

3. Have students compare their journals to Sarah Emery's.

**Follow-up:** Have students compare pressures on today's youth with those of children in the past.

Ask students to check with grandparents or other relatives who might have kept diaries and would be willing to come in and share them with the class.

**Adaptation:** Students could write daily or periodic journals based on academic topics being studied.

# Writing a Ballad

**Objective:**  The students will each write a ballad about the Battle of the Alamo.

**Materials:**  March 1982 issue of COBBLESTONE, paper, pencils.

**Procedure:**  After reading through the above issue of COBBLESTONE, discuss the personalities involved on both sides in the Battle of the Alamo.

Tell students they will each be writing a ballad about one or more people involved in the battle.

Explain that a ballad tells a story in verse. It is frequently made into a song and is one of the oldest forms of poetry and music. Ballads were first used among people who could not read or write. They told and sang stories that were passed down orally through generations. Ballads frequently follow a format using a four-line stanza in which the second and fourth lines rhyme. Ballads do vary in their rhyming patterns, though, so the students should simply try to be consistent with the rhyme and rhythm as they develop their poetic stories.

Read aloud the poem on page 40 of the March 1982 issue of COBBLE-STONE. It is a good example of a ballad on the Alamo.

(Before students begin their ballads, you might develop a "word bank" on the board. Students brainstorm by naming as many words that relate to the Alamo as they can, including names of people. The list generally helps students in their writing.)

Give students paper and have them write their ballads.

**Follow-up:**  Have students read their ballads to the class.

Have students draw pictures to illustrate their ballads.

Find ballads in literature to read to the class.

**Adaptation:**  Students could use other forms of poetry to write about famous persons or events.

# A Pictograph on World Wheat Production

**Objective:**

The students will each use a pictograph to answer questions about world wheat production.

**Materials:**

April 1982 issue of COBBLESTONE, Blackline Master #25, pencils.

**Procedure:**

Ask students whether they remember which country originally brought wheat to America. The Spanish explorers brought wheat to our country, along with many other things and animals we have today (COBBLESTONE, March 1981).

Talk about the importance of wheat in our diets. Even back in our early history, a gristmill to grind grain into flour was frequently one of the first buildings to be erected.

Discuss the role of wheat today. Either read aloud to the students or have them read "The Russian Grain Embargo" on pages 36–40 of the April 1982 issue. Talk about the political value of wheat.

Give each student a copy of Blackline Master #25 and explain the parts of the pictograph. Be sure students understand that they must check the key to see the value of one symbol on the graph before they begin.

Correct the graphs together if students were uncertain of how to do the questions. Show them how they should count by tens to find how much wheat each country produced.

**Follow-up:**

Have students make diagrams of the actual parts of a wheat kernel. Discuss the nutritional value of these parts.

**Adaptation:**

Pictographs help students use symbols as visual aids to make comparisons. Students might make their own pictographs, deciding what information they want to compare, choosing a symbol to use on the graph, and developing questions for other students to answer.

# Using a Product Map: Natural Resources of California

**Objective:**    The students will each use a product map of California to answer questions about the state's natural resources.

**Materials:**    May 1982 issue of COBBLESTONE, Blackline Master #26, pencils.

**Procedure:**    Do a brainstorming session with students by having them write down things they associate with the state of California. Give them two minutes to write everything they can think of.

Next, have students share items from their lists. Write them on the board and have students explain why they associate the items with California.

On another section of the board, label a column "Natural Resources." Ask students if they can explain what natural resources are and have them identify any that appear on the brainstorming list. Write these in the Natural Resources column. You might also ask them to explain what manmade resources are and have them identify any that appear on the brainstorming list.

Give each student a copy of Blackline Master #26 and review the directions. Also read aloud the names of natural resources that appear in the key and be sure they understand what they mean.

Have students answer questions about California's natural resources.

**Follow-up:**    Ask students whether they can identify natural resources that are not products (for example, mountains, rivers, and lakes). Discuss the need and reasons for protection of our natural resources. Include in the discussion ways these resources can be harmed over short or long periods of time and how this can be prevented.

**Adaptation:**    Product maps are good tools to help students learn about resources from different states and countries. Students could research and make their own product maps about places they are studying.

# Drawing Different Routes on a Map: The Beaver Trade

**Objective:** The students will each be given a map on which they will draw three possible routes used by early fur traders.

**Materials:** June 1982 issue of COBBLESTONE, Blackline Master #27, pencils.

**Procedure:** After reading through the issue, discuss the importance of the beaver trade in the early 1800s. Ask what types of businesses are important today. Compare these two periods. Discuss economic changes over time and their causes. Another good topic for this discussion would be the change in agriculture in this country.

Give each student a copy of Blackline Master #27 and carefully review the directions. Before they begin work, pronounce the names of the various rivers and lakes and have the students locate them on the map. This will help them to follow the written directions for drawing the trade routes.

**Follow-up:** Talk about the fur industry today. Discuss the concern about killing animals for their skins. Name the baby seal and the whale as examples of animals that have groups of people working for their protection. Ask students how they feel about the subject. Discuss why public opinion and concern would differ between today and the early 1800s.

**Adaptation:** Students could trace routes on a map to show how someone has moved through his or her life or how a group has traveled from one place to another.

# Designing a Brand

**Objective:** The students will design and name their own brands.

**Materials:** July 1982 issue of COBBLESTONE, Blackline Master #28, pencils.

**Procedure:** After reading through the issue, discuss what life was like for a cowboy in the 1800s. Talk about the cowboys of today and their lifestyles. (Many make their money in rodeo events.)

Review the history of branding cattle. Ask why the numbers and types of brands increased.

Give each student a copy of Blackline Master #28. Have them write their name and the date on it, then ask them to look at the upper section of the worksheet. This part is taken from the July 1982 issue of COBBLE-STONE. It explains how to read a brand, then gives examples of brands for students to name. As a large group, review the brands when the students have finished.

In the bottom section is a space for each student to design his or her own brand. Have them think it over, make a large drawing of it, then cut the worksheet along the dotted line. They should write the name of their brand on the back of the paper. Collect the brands.

**Follow-up:** Make a bulletin board displaying the students' brands and have people guess their names. They can check by looking on the back of the papers.

**Adaptation:** Students can express their individuality by designing their own flags, flowers, trees, and so on.

# A Circus Poster

**Objective:**   The students will each design an advertisement poster for a circus featured in the August 1982 issue of COBBLESTONE.

**Materials:**   August 1982 issue of COBBLESTONE, construction paper, stencils, pencils, rulers, coloring tools.

**Procedure:**   After reading through the above issue of COBBLESTONE, ask students to name animals or things they associate with a circus. List these on the board.

Explain to students that they are to imagine they have been hired to design an advertisement poster for one of the circuses described in the August 1982 issue of COBBLESTONE.

Ask what type of information should go on a poster. As a group, make up a fictitious date, time, and place for the circus. Write this information on the board for students to use.

Next, ask students what makes an effective poster. (Discuss features such as size, readability, color, creativity, and artwork.) Tell them to keep these in mind as they create their posters.

You might want to discuss and show examples of early posters, advertisements, and news sources. Ask students to check their homes for old catalogues, newspapers, or pictures they could share with the class.

Give each student a large sheet of construction paper and have them design their posters.

**Follow-up:**   Display the students' posters.

Read aloud William Saroyan's story "The Circus Comes to Town," featured in the above issue of COBBLESTONE. (Be sure students have not read this before.) When you reach the point in the story where the boys are in Mr. Dawson's office to find out what is going to happen to them for skipping school (page 29), stop reading. Have students orally predict what they think will happen to the boys. Then finish the story.

**Adaptation:**   Making posters draws on a variety of skills. Students could make them to promote school or community events or causes. They could also advertise a favorite book.

# A Classroom Bill of Rights

**Objective:** As a large group, the students will decide on their classroom's "Bill of Rights."

**Materials:** September 1982 issue of COBBLESTONE, large sheet of paper, markers.

**Procedure:** After reading the article "The Constitution of the United States" in the September 1982 issue of COBBLESTONE, discuss why a country needs a constitution. Ask what it does for us.

Ask students why they think our Constitution is still working.

Discuss the meaning of an amendment. Explain that the first ten amendments to our Constitution are known as the Bill of Rights, which guarantees the rights of individuals. They are as follows:

1. Freedom of Religion, Speech, and the Press; Rights of Assembly and Petition
2. Right to Bear Arms
3. Housing of Soldiers (Soldiers cannot by quartered without the owner's consent.)
4. Search and Arrest Warrants (Today, a warrant is necessary before a search or an arrest can be carried out.)
5. Rights in Criminal Cases (A grand jury indictment is necessary; there can be no double jeopardy; and no one can be forced to testify against himself or herself.)
6. Right to a Fair Trial (A speedy public trial by an impartial jury is guaranteed.)
7. Rights in Civil Cases (Trial by jury is guaranteed in civil cases where the value in controversy exceeds twenty dollars.)
8. Bails, Fines, and Punishments (There can be no excessive bail or fines and no cruel and unusual punishment.)

9. Rights Retained by the People (People have rights other than those guaranteed here.)
10. Powers Retained by the States and the People (This was written to protect States' rights.)

Explain to students that they are going to decide on their classroom's "Bill of Rights," which will help guarantee individual rights within the room. Have students give suggestions, then vote and choose the number of rights you wish to have for the room. Post them on a large piece of paper.

**Follow-up:**    Use the activity on pages 26–29 in the above issue. It presents situations, then asks students if rights have been violated.

**Adaptation:**    In current events, compare our individual rights to those in other countries.

# Sightseeing Along the Erie Canal

**Objective:**    The students will research and orally present facts about towns or cities located along the route of the Erie Canal.

**Materials:**    October 1982 issue of COBBLESTONE, reference books that include information on the Erie Canal, bulletin board space, construction paper, coloring tools.

**Procedure:**    Prior to starting the activity, trace the route of the Erie Canal and print the names of towns or cities located along it on the bulletin board. Have a student make a model of a canalboat that can move along the bulletin board route of the canal. Place the canalboat at Albany.

Explain to students that they are to pretend they could follow the Erie Canal across New York State today. As a large group, examine the route and the towns and cities along it. Assign individuals or small groups of students a particular town or city to research. Explain that each day, the canalboat will move to the next city or town, and the students who completed research on that place will present their information orally to the rest of the class. The boat remains at that town or city until the following day, when it is moved by a student to the next place. (Students could also draw pictures that show something about the town or city next to its name.)

**Follow-up:**    Discuss the role of the Erie Canal in our westward expansion.

Ask students why they think the Erie Canal lost its popularity.

**Adaptation:**    Having students research cities along a particular route is an interesting way to study a state or region. They could also study other important waterways in this country or the world.

# Frederic Remington's Art

**Objective:**    The students will each choose a picture of one of Remington's paintings or drawings from the November 1982 issue of COBBLESTONE, then write a story about it.

**Materials:**    November 1982 issue of COBBLESTONE, reference books on Frederic Remington, paper, pencils.

**Procedure:**    This activity would make a good learning center where students work in their free time.

Place the materials listed above at the learning center.

Also place these directions at the center:

1. Read through this issue of COBBLESTONE.

2. Choose a picture of one of Remington's paintings or drawings. Study it until you get a mental picture of a story that might be taking place.

3. On a piece of paper, write your name, the date, and the title of the work of art you have chosen.

4. Using paragraph form, write your story of what you see happening in Remington's art.

5. Proofread your story and turn it in.

**Follow-up:**    Have students share their stories orally.

Ask how Remington's art could help someone learn about our past.

**Adaptation:**    Show pictures of famous works of art to the students. Have them write stories about them. They could also look up information about the artists.

You could establish an "Artist of the Month" center and feature a different artist each month by putting out biographical information and books that show examples of the artist's work.

# Plotting Family Origins

**Objective:** The students will find out which line of their ancestries immigrated to America, then plot the countries of origin on a world map.

**Materials:** December 1982 issue of COBBLESTONE, large world map to put on a bulletin board, string or yarn, pins, paper, markers.

**Procedure:** Pin up a large world map on the bulletin board. (If you do not have one, use a projector to trace one on a piece of butcher paper.)

Above it, use your own method to put up a title such as "Our Family Origins."

Discuss the meanings of the words "immigrate" and "emigrate." Use the time line on pages 6–7 in the above issue to discuss the history of immigration in this country. Tell the class we are a land of immigrants and ask them what it means.

As a homework assignment, have students write down the line of ancestry (if possible, on both mother's and father's side) that immigrated to America and the country from which they came.

Have students cut slips of paper that measure one inch by two inches. Have them print their names on the slips, then pin the slips on an area of the bulletin board outside the world map. Then have them connect yarn from their names to their ancestors' original countries.

**Follow-up:** After the students have identified their countries of origin, develop oral questions that help them to draw conclusions about the map. For example, ask from which country most of the immigrants to this country came and from which country the fewest came.

**Adaptation:** Students could plot countries of origin of famous Americans who immigrated to this country.

# Locating Countries on a World Map

**Objective:**     The students will each use a world map to identify some of the countries from which America's immigrants came.

**Materials:**     January 1983 issue of COBBLESTONE, Blackline Master #29, pencils.

**Procedure:**     Have students name as many nationalities as they can. Discuss various customs, languages, and dress of other cultures. Ask why the term "melting pot" is used when referring to America.

Ask students if they can give examples of contributions made by immigrants to this country. Allow them time to investigate individual and ethnic contributions to America.

After reading through the January 1983 issue of COBBLESTONE, give each student a copy of Blackline Master #29 and review the directions. The students will find and color the home countries of some of our immigrants.

**Follow-up:**     Have the students identify customs of immigrants from other countries shown on the map, then ask them to color these nations. Also have students come up with their own questions.

Discuss the immigration issue our country faces today. Who are most of this country's immigrants now? Ask what an illegal alien is. Discuss why they come to this country and the problems this can create. Ask students to watch for news on this topic.

**Adaptation:**     Locating and coloring countries are skills that can be used in various academic topics, especially social studies and current events.

# How Would I Have Felt?

**Objective:** The students will each write a paragraph describing how they might have felt if they had been a slave.

**Materials:** February 1983 issue of COBBLESTONE, reference books on slavery, paper, pencils.

**Procedure:** After reading through the February 1983 issue of COBBLESTONE on black history, discuss the slavery issue with students.

Ask them who favored it and why. Then ask who opposed it and why.

Have students examine the illustration on page 6, which shows a slave ship. Ask them to imagine what it would have been like traveling from Africa to America on such a ship.

Discuss the effects of slavery on the personal and family lives of slaves.

Tell students they are to imagine what it would have felt like to have been a slave. Then ask them to write a paragraph expressing these feelings.

**Follow-up:** Ask students if they had lived in a time when slavery was legal, how they might have reacted toward the issue.

Discuss people and events in black history, especially the struggle for equal rights in the United States.

Have students write and perform a short play involving the slavery issue. In this way, students can actually demonstrate how they might have reacted if they had been involved with slavery.

**Adaptation:** Helping students empathize with another's situation can lead to better understanding. This type of activity causes the students to imagine how another person might have felt and to see another's point of view.

You might also have students investigate slavery in other countries.

# Medical Milestones

**Objective:** The students will be able to match a person to the medical milestone for which he or she is responsible.

**Materials:** March 1983 issue of COBBLESTONE, Blackline Master #30, pencils.

**Procedure:** After reading through the issue, ask students whether they can think of any dreaded diseases that still wipe out large numbers of people in our country or the world.

Discuss the concept of vaccination and talk about how it has prevented people from contracting diseases that struck earlier generations. Suggest that students interview their grandparents to see if they recall any epidemics and what health care was like when they were young.

Give each student a copy of Blackline Master #30 and review the directions. (You might wish to have the above discussion, then allow students to complete this activity in a learning center or in their free time. They might wish to do further research on some of these or other topics.)

**Follow-up:** Have students look up information on early medicinal practices such as bloodletting and blistering.

You might spend some time studying and investigating "quackery." Students could search through magazines for advertisements that are misleading. It is important for them to learn that just because a claim is made in print (even with testimonials and alleged proof of success), it is not necessarily true and reliable.

You might also look into different medical practices in the world and how attitudes toward medicine differ.

**Adaptation:** Students could match the names of people with their accomplishments in a variety of academic or current topics.

# A Visit to a Shaker Community

**Objective:** The students will each be given an imaginary letter written by a visitor to a Shaker community, and they will identify incorrect statements about Shakers.

**Materials:** April 1983 issue of COBBLESTONE, Blackline Master #31, pencils.

**Procedure:** After reading through the issue, discuss what it means to be a Shaker. Ask students to describe what life might be like if they were to join a community. Review Shaker views on marriage, politics, and work.

Discuss the contributions of the Shakers. Ask students whether they have any Shaker furnishings in their homes.

Give each student a copy of Blackline Master #31. It asks students to read an imaginary letter written by a visitor to a Shaker village. The letter contains incorrect statements about Shakers. The students are to read the letter, decide which statements do not belong, then cross them out.

**Follow-up:** Have students complete the activity, then go over the letter as a large group. Have students give reasons why certain statements would not be true of Shakers.

Another follow-up idea would be to have students pretend they are visiting a Shaker community, then ask them to write a letter to a friend describing the Shakers' lifestyle.

**Adaptation:** Students could do this type of activity with other groups that follow particular guidelines in their daily lives.

# Making a Braille Alphabet

**Objective:** The students will each construct a Braille alphabet, then compose a sentence for others to read.

**Materials:** May 1983 issue of COBBLESTONE, Blackline Master #32, cardboard, split peas, pencils, paste.

**Procedure:** Discuss the term "handicap" with the students. Ask them which handicaps Helen Keller had. How did she overcome them?

Discuss the sign-language alphabet for deaf people. Ask if any students know how to use it.

Ask if anyone has seen a Braille alphabet. Have someone describe it. Which of our five senses does it use?

Give each student a copy of Blackline Master #32 and review the directions. It would be best if they pasted the sheet on a piece of cardboard before beginning. They will paste split peas on the given dots to make the raised alphabet.

Below the alphabet is a space for students to construct a short sentence. They can then trade papers and try to read each other's sentences.

**Follow-up:** Discuss how Helen Keller developed her talents in spite of her handicaps.

Ask students if they can think of other famous people who excelled in spite of a handicap. (Beethoven was deaf when he finished his *Ninth Symphony*. He never heard it, but had to rely on remarks of friends.)

**Adaptation:** Students could study other alphabets such as those from ancient civilizations or those of a modern foreign language. They could attempt to write words, phrases, or sentences using the alphabets they study. (See "Sequoya and the Talking Leaves" in the February 1983 issue of COBBLESTONE.)

# A Personal Time Capsule

**Objective:**    At the beginning of the school year, the students will each answer five specific questions about themselves. They will then reexamine their answers in June and note any changes.

**Materials:**    June 1983 issue of COBBLESTONE, paper, pencils, large jar or other container with lid.

**Procedure:**    After reading through the above issue, ask students how the study of archaeology is like solving a mystery. Discuss with them the importance of this field. Ask what types of things we can learn from an earlier age.

Ask students what kinds of changes have occurred in their lives. Discuss physical changes, but also stress changes in interests and goals. Ask how many students can remember their favorite food or pastime when they were five years old.

Discuss the purpose of a time capsule. (See the January 1984 issue of COBBLESTONE.) Explain to students that they are going to make a personal time capsule. While archaeologists study changes that occur over long periods of time, the students are going to be able to examine changes within a school year.

Directions for personal time capsule:

1. Write the following five questions on the board, then have students answer them on small sheets of paper.

   1. What is your present height? (a good math activity)
   2. Who is your favorite singer?
   3. What is your favorite book?
   4. What is your favorite pastime?
   5. What three goals over which you have control would you like to work on this year? These goals can be in the areas of academic, self-improvement, or personal relationship skills.

2. Put the students' responses in a sealed jar or container and put it away until the end of the school year.

3. At the end of the school year, give students their response sheets and have them note any changes.

**Follow-up:** Ask students which questions were most likely to show change. Find out how many students were able to work toward specific self-improvement goals once they had identified them and put them in writing.

**Adaptation:** Have students set a new self-improvement or academic goal each month.

# Pourquoi Stories

**Objective:**

The students will each choose an animal and write a story about how it got a particular feature.

**Materials:**

July 1983 issue of COBBLESTONE, paper, pencils.

**Procedure:**

Read some of the stories from the July 1983 issue of COBBLESTONE, "Folklore: Stories and More."

Discuss the development of stories that explain how an animal got a particular feature, such as a skunk's stripe or odor, a tiger's stripes, or an owl's hoot. Emphasize that this type of story is imaginary and should be exaggerated or humorous. It might also show how an animal was taught a lesson. As a large group, choose an animal and develop a story together.

Explain that the students are to write their own stories of how an animal got a particular feature. Tell them these are called "pourquoi stories" because they tell why an animal looks or sounds as it does. (*Pourquoi* is the French word for "why.")

Have a brainstorming session in which students name all the animals they can, along with the features peculiar to them. List several on the board. Have each student choose an animal and write a story.

**Follow-up:**

The students could read their stories aloud and listen for the most creative explanations of how animals got their traits.

Compile all the stories into a class book.

**Adaptation:**

Students could tell stories orally, making them up as they went along. One student could begin, then others could take over at different points. After a set time period, someone would end the story.

# Unscrambling a Public Works Message

**Objective:** The students will unscramble letters to find vocabulary words that lead to a message about public works.

**Materials:** August 1983 issue of COBBLESTONE, Blackline Master #33, pencils.

**Procedure:** After reading through the issue, have students describe what is included in public works.

Ask which of these we take for granted and how we would miss them if they were taken away.

Discuss how society's needs have changed and how our increased population has affected the demands on public works.

If possible, arrange to take the class to its town's Department of Public Works. (This could also be a follow-up activity.)

Give each student a copy of Blackline Master #33 and review the directions. The students will unscramble the letters to find words related to public works. They will then unscramble another set of letters to answer a specific question.

**Follow-up:** Ask students to describe the public works system in their own town or city.

Ask students which forms of public transportation they have used. Discuss the advantages and disadvantages of different types of public transportation.

There could be a cleanup day at school or in the town or city, and students could help by making posters to recruit workers.

**Adaptation:** Unscrambling letters to make words is a good vocabulary activity that would fit most academic topics.

# A Television News Report

**Objective:** The students will each prepare an oral two-minute news report on any person or event from the Revolutionary War period.

**Materials:** September 1983 issue of COBBLESTONE, reference books on the Revolutionary War and people and events of that time period, paper, pencils.

**Procedure:** Have students read through the September 1983 issue of COBBLESTONE and other reference books on people and events from the Revolutionary War period. Suggest they check on artists, musicians, and human interest stories as well as Revolutionary War incidents.

Ask students how people knew what was happening in the war, since there was no television or radio. Ask them how we receive news today.

Discuss how television might have affected the Revolutionary War. Ask students to be specific in their responses. Ask students what an evening broadcast might have been like if there had been television.

Explain that they are to pretend there was television back then and that they are each going to prepare a two-minute news report on any person or event from the Revolutionary War period. Tell them to consider who, what, when, where, and how when they write a draft of their report.

Have a few students give reports each day at a specified news time.

**Follow-up:** Ask students which events or persons they think would have received the most attention from television. Have them explain why.

Discuss how different news programs today can give different views of the same news. Stress the importance of objectivity in reporting on people and events.

**Adaptation:** A newscast format for oral reports could be used for a variety of academic topics.

# A Jazzy Crossword Puzzle

**Objective:** The students will each complete a crossword puzzle using vocabulary words related to jazz.

**Materials:** October 1983 issue of COBBLESTONE, Blackline Master #34, pencils.

**Procedure:** Read aloud "Jazz Ingredients" to the students. (It is on pages 10 and 11 of the October 1983 issue of COBBLESTONE.) Talk about terms such as blues, ragtime, and rhythm. Discuss why jazz is a unique form of American music.

After students have read through the issue, highlight the different personalities of jazz. Talk over the particular aspect of jazz that made them famous.

Ask students if they have ever seen a live jazz performance. Talk about the way feelings are brought out through the music.

Give each student a copy of Blackline Master #34 and have each complete the puzzle.

**Follow-up:** Discuss the different types of instruments used in jazz. Ask if any students play these instruments or if any hope to play them in the future.

Play some jazz recordings and ask students to identify the different instruments.

**Adaptation:** Crossword puzzles are good tools for reinforcing vocabulary words from any academic topic.

# Finding the Key Word

**Objective:** The students will each be given a set of questions, and they must identify the key word they would use to find the answers in an encyclopedia or other reference book.

**Materials:** November 1983 issue of COBBLESTONE, Blackline Master #35, pencils.

**Procedure:** Have students name as many things as they can that could be found in a library.

Ask which are their favorite sections of the library and have them explain why. Talk about other things a library offers besides books. (Many libraries offer programs, contests, activities, and special events.)

Discuss the reference section. Ask for a definition of a reference book. Have the students explain how to use a table of contents and an index. Ask which is more specific and which they would use to see whether information on a particular topic was included in the book.

Explain how you determine the key word to find information on a particular subject. (Remind students to use a person's last name when looking up information.)

Give each student a copy of Blackline Master #35 and review the directions.

**Follow-up:** Arrange to meet with the librarian of your local or city library and take an inventory of its facilities, programs, exhibits, and hours.

Arrange a time to take the class to the library on a regular basis to familiarize students with all its aspects.

**Adaptation:** Determining the key word to locate information is an essential skill in all academic areas.

# How Well Did You Listen?

**Objective:** The students will answer multiple-choice questions after listening to an article titled "Living in the Dust Bowl."

**Materials:** December 1983 issue of COBBLESTONE, Blackline Master #36, pencils.

**Procedure:** Explain to students that you are going to read an article called "Living in the Dust Bowl." They are to listen very carefully because they will take a listening test when the reading is finished.

Discuss how to focus and concentrate on listening. Suggest that they watch you read and make mental pictures of what they hear.

Read the article "Living in the Dust Bowl" on pages 22–27 in the December 1983 issue of COBBLESTONE.

Give each student a copy of Blackline Master #36. Read the questions and answers once. The students are to circle the letter of the correct answer. (Be sure they write their names and the date on the test.)

Have students turn in the tests.

**Follow-up:** Once the tests are collected, go over each question so students have immediate feedback.

Ask if students have listening hints for each other.

On the subject of the Dust Bowl, discuss the plight of farmers and the determination required by individuals and families to remain throughout that devastating period.

Discuss conservation measures that protect soil, water, forests, and other natural resources. Ask what would happen if people did not care about these resources.

**Adaptation:** Regular listening tests that integrate material the class is studying can help improve listening skills and the students' comprehension of the subject matter.

# Making Predictions

**Objective:** The students will each make ten predictions of what life might be like one hundred years from now.

**Materials:** January 1984 issue of COBBLESTONE, paper, pencils.

**Procedure:** Read aloud "Predictions from 1900" in the January 1984 issue of COBBLESTONE.

Discuss the predictions. How many came close to predicting life today? Which ones did not?

Explain to the students that they are to imagine what life will be like one hundred years from now. They should think over and write ten predictions of what life will be like then.

**Follow-up:** Have students read their predictions aloud. Discuss those that are most likely to happen.

Ask students if they think people who lived 150 years ago would be amazed at our world today.

Have students share their favorite science fiction stories or books. Ask if they think the story or book could become nonfiction in the future.

**Adaptation:** Students could make predictions related to specific topics in science, math, social studies, or current political affairs.

# Letter to the Editor

**Objective:** The students will each write a letter to the editor giving their reactions to the "Trail of Tears."

**Materials:** February 1984 issue of COBBLESTONE, paper, pencils.

**Procedure:** Read aloud "The Trail of Tears" in the February 1984 issue of COBBLESTONE.

Discuss how the Cherokee Indians were moved from Georgia to Oklahoma. Ask students how they feel about the treatment of the Indians.

Ask what Daniel Webster's reaction was. If more people had spoken up earlier on the Indians' behalf, do the students think it might have made a difference?

Explain to students that today we can write to the newspaper if we have an opinion on a matter. This is a letter to the editor, and it is printed for all to read. Usually a person writes such a letter when he or she feels strongly about a particular matter. It can be positive or negative.

Tell students they are to write a letter to the editor as if they had experienced some part of the Cherokee Indians' move. Tell them to give specific reasons for their feelings. When writing their letters, have them use "Dear Editor:" for the greeting.

**Follow-up:** Have students share their letters orally or put them on the bulletin board for all to read. Discuss which letters might have influenced public opinion on the treatment of the Cherokee Indians.

Discuss how it might feel to be uprooted from your home and moved to a strange place far away.

**Adaptation:** Students could write letters to the editor to actual newspapers giving their opinions on local or national topics.

Read actual letters to the editor from a local or national paper. Have students react to others' opinions.

# Prized Possessions

**Objective:**   The students will each list three personal possessions they would not sell if they lived in a "depression," and they will defend why they would keep those particular items.

**Materials:**   March 1984 issue of COBBLESTONE, paper, pencils.

**Procedure:**   After reading through the above issue, discuss the Depression era. Have students ask their grandparents or other adults what it was like to have lived during the Depression. Ask students to share what they learned in their interviews.

If possible, invite someone who lived during the Depression into class to share what it was like. It is important for students to understand the hardships most people experienced.

Ask if the name suited the era. Have students give reasons for their responses. Discuss some of the hardships mentioned in the issue.

Emphasize that many people struggled simply to buy food and shelter and that there was no money for "extras." Next, ask students to imagine what it might be like for them to live in a depression era. Tell them they are to pretend that the family must sell most of its belongings for food money, but their parents have said they may each choose three items to keep.

Tell students this activity requires very serious thought. They must think over which three items they would keep and why. Have them write their three "prized possessions" and their defense for keeping them on a sheet of paper.

**Follow-up:**   Set up a panel of students to whom other class members will orally defend their reasons for keeping their three chosen items. The members of the panel may ask questions, then decide whether each student's choices were justifiable.

Suggest that students interview adults who lived during the Depression to find out if it still affects their lives.

**Adaptation:**   Having students think over their priorities is a useful exercise. It might also be beneficial to have students consider how their choices affect others.

# A Whaling Diorama

**Objective:** The students will each construct a diorama depicting a scene from the whaling era.

**Materials:** April 1984 issue of COBBLESTONE, shoe boxes, construction paper, paste, paper, pencils, coloring tools, other individual materials.

**Procedure:** Have students read through the above issue.

Discuss the various aspects of whaling and what it might have been like to have been a crew member on a whaleboat.

Tell students they are going to make a diorama depicting a whaling scene. Explain that a diorama is a box that exhibits a three-dimensional scene about a specific topic or event.

Students will have to bring in a small box; a shoe box is ideal.

Tell them to plan a three-dimensional scene showing something about whaling.

Tell them they can draw on the sides of the box, then paste the rest of their scene in it.

Explain that, as a last step, they need to write a title and a one-paragraph description about their dioramas. These descriptions will be placed next to the boxes when they are put on display.

**Follow-up:** Put the dioramas on display and invite parents and other classes to see them.

**Adaptation:** Dioramas could be made for a favorite book or other social studies or science topics.

# First Prize: A Day With Mark Twain

**Objective:** The students will each write a paragraph telling how they would choose to spend a day with Mark Twain.

**Materials:** May 1984 issue of COBBLESTONE, Blackline Master #37, pencils.

**Procedure:** Explain to students that they have each won a prize in an imaginary contest that will allow them to spend a day with Mark Twain.

After reading through the COBBLESTONE issue, discuss the various aspects of Mark Twain's life, including his jobs and his homes. Talk about the different periods of his life—as a boy rafting down the Mississippi, a newspaper reporter, a steamboat pilot, and a writer.

Explain to students that they are going to write about spending a day with Mark Twain. Ask them to choose a time period, then think over where and how they would spend their special day. Have them think over what they would like to talk about with the author and what they hope to learn from him.

Once they have thought this through, give each student a copy of Blackline Master #37 and review the directions.

**Follow-up:** Have students read their compositions orally.

Have students draw an illustration of their activity with Mark Twain.

Discuss how to make decisions when you have a limited time frame. Do students feel they planned a good and productive day with Mark Twain?

**Adaptation:** Students could write what it would be like to spend a day with any notable person. They may even wish to meet with a few people (such as political leaders) to ask pertinent questions regarding their influence on world decisions.

# A Bar Graph: Which Program Would Help You?

**Objective:**    The students will each make a bar graph using information on which types of computer programs would help in academic subjects.

**Materials:**    June 1984 issue of COBBLESTONE, Blackline Master #38, pencils.

**Procedure:**    Discuss the history of computers with students. Explain that only recently have the numbers and kinds of computers increased dramatically.

Talk over computer terms such as input, output, disk, terminal, software, and byte. See how many students are familiar with these terms and whether they can explain them.

Talk about uses of computers. How can schools use them best? Ask how students think computers help them learn. Talk over the advantages and disadvantages of computers in schools.

Explain to students that they are going to make a bar graph. Give them each a copy of Blackline Master #38 and read the directions with them. Read over the tally. Tell them to answer the questions below the box, then use the information to make the bar graph at the bottom of the worksheet.

**Follow-up:**    Students who know how to use a computer could design their own programs for topics they are studying.

Students could visit a local business and have someone explain how the computer works and how the company uses it in the business.

**Adaptation:**    Students could tally classmates' opinions on a variety of subjects, then make a bar graph showing the results. (They could choose topics such as favorite foods, songs, and games.)

# Classroom Olympics

**Objective:**   The students will be given sets of criteria that they must meet to qualify for medals in five academic areas.

**Materials:**   August 1984 issue of COBBLESTONE, construction paper, scissors, plain paper, markers.

**Procedure:**   This is a bulletin board activity that encourages students to go beyond the daily requirements of academic work.

Preparation:

- Cut out five rings of different-colored paper and staple them on the bulletin board in the pattern of the Olympic Rings. (See the above issue for this pattern.)

- Cut out the letters for a title, such as "Be an Academic Olympian," and put the title on the board.

- Inside each ring, write an academic label and list the criteria you would like each student to meet to qualify for a medal. (You might choose math, reading, science, social studies, and writing for your five areas.) You must decide which subject areas and sets of criteria best suit your group of students. An example of one ring might be the following:

  Writing—To qualify for a medal, you must write a haiku, a
    limerick, a biographical sketch, and a humorous story.

Explanation:

- Tell students that during this marking period, you are going to hold a "Classroom Olympics." Explain the five rings and the sets of criteria. Give students a date by which all work must be completed. If the students meet the criteria, they qualify for a medal.

- When the deadline arrives, evaluate the students' work, then choose the students who deserve the gold, silver, and bronze medals. (You may design either a medal or a certificate that is appropriate for your level of students.) Students who qualified might also receive some sort of an honorable mention award for their effort.

- Hold an awards ceremony in your room or in front of the student body to give participating students recognition for their work.

**Follow-up:** Discuss the history of and changes in the Olympic Games.

**Adaptation:** Olympic events could also be designed for areas such as music, art, physical education, citizenship, and self-improvement.

# Outlining: Starting a Nation

**Objective:**    The students will organize the content of specific magazine articles into outline form.

**Materials:**    September 1984 issue of COBBLESTONE, paper, pencils.

**Procedure:**    This activity helps students organize important information from a magazine article into outline form. It could be an individual, small-group, or large-group lesson.

First, review how to outline with the students. Remind them to use Roman numerals for main headings, capital letters for subtopics, and Arabic numerals for supporting details. Write the pattern shown below on the board:

    I.  First main heading
       A. Subtopic
       B. Subtopic
          1. Supporting detail
          2. Supporting detail

    II.  Second main heading
       A. Subtopic
       B. Subtopic
          1. Supporting detail
          2. Supporting detail

Have students note the indenting pattern and the use of periods and capital letters. Also remind them that their outlines are to follow the order in which material is presented in the magazine article.

In the next part of the lesson, assign articles from the above issue of COBBLESTONE for students to read, then outline.

**Follow-up:**    Display students' outlines on a bulletin board with the 1984 issue of COBBLESTONE at its center.

Have students write their own versions of the articles, using their outlines as guides.

**Adaptation:**    Students could outline material from various textbooks, or they could generate their own outlines from notes taken for a research paper.

# What Is Your Theory?

**Objective:**   The students will work in small groups to study, then present the different theories of who first came to America.

**Materials:**   October 1984 issue of COBBLESTONE, other materials to be determined by the small groups.

**Procedure:**   This activity will culminate in a mock conference where students will present the different theories on who first came to America.

First, discuss the meaning of a theory. Ask whether a theory is rigid. Discuss how theories are developed and how and why they might change. Talk about the reasons for possible resistance to change.

Next, divide the class into seven groups. Each group should then be assigned one of the following titles: Indians, Phoenicians, Vikings, Columbus, Irish, Chinese, Welsh.

The above issue of COBBLESTONE contains articles on each of the groups or individuals and how they came or might have come to America. Have each group of students read its assigned article, then ask them to develop a presentation to try and persuade others to accept the theory that it was their group or individual who first came to America.

Hold a mock conference and ask each group to present its theory. The students might prepare charts, maps, or other visual aids to help them in their presentation.

**Follow-up:**   Discuss which group presented the most persuasive argument.

Have students read about past theories that were changed when new evidence was discovered (for example, Copernicus) and ask them to investigate the impact on the world and the reactions of people at the time.

**Adaptation:**   When studying issues that encompass several viewpoints, a mock conference is a good method to allow students to present different schools of thought.

# Dear Senator...

**Objective:** The students will discuss a current political issue, then write to a United States senator for his or her opinion on the matter.

**Materials:** November 1984 issue of COBBLESTONE, paper, pencils, envelopes, stamps, *Congressional Directory*.

**Procedure:** After reading through the above issue of the magazine, discuss the responsibilities of a United States senator. Then talk about what one might observe during a session in the Senate. Ask what topics might be discussed. Have students explain the meaning of filibuster and its purpose in the Senate.

Next, discuss a current national issue. Then read aloud to students or have them carefully read "How to Write Your United States Senator" on pages 39–40 in the above issue of COBBLESTONE.

Explain to students that they will each write a letter to a United States senator and ask for his or her opinion on a particular issue (to be decided by the class).

Review the correct form for writing a business letter. Then have each student choose a senator to whom to write. (The *Congressional Directory* can usually be found in the reference section of the library; it contains names and addresses of the United States senators.)

**Follow-up:** When a student receives a response, it should be read aloud to the class.

Have students display all responses on a bulletin board.

**Adaptation:** Have students write to their state senators or representatives about a particular issue.

# Design Your Own Flying Machine

**Objective:**　The students will each design an original flying machine.

**Materials:**　December 1984 issue of COBBLESTONE, drawing paper, coloring tools, writing paper, pencils.

**Procedure:**　After reading through the above issue, discuss the history of aviation. Ask why it is such a fascinating topic.

Have students look through books (both fact and fiction) to find pictures of interesting flying machines. Ask them to share any they might find.

Next, explain to students that they are to imagine they are inventors who are going to design original flying machines. Tell them they are to assume that materials are not a problem; they can be as creative as they wish.

Give each student a sheet of drawing paper and ask them to design their machines in detail. When they are finished, have each student explain his or her machine to the rest of the class.

**Follow-up:**　Have the students write creative stories about an imaginary voyage they took on their flying machines.

Display the designs and stories on a bulletin board.

Have interested students complete further research on the Wright brothers.

**Adaptation:**　The students could design other original modes of transportation and write descriptions of how they operate.

Then & Now: Comparing Maps of the Same Area
January 1980 Issue
Blackline Master #5

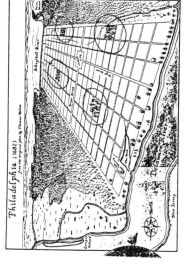

Philadelphia (1682) from the original plan by Thomas Holme

Philadelphia Today

## Then & Now: Comparing Maps of the Same Area

**Directions:** Fill in the blanks.

1. Find "Center City" on the 1682 map. A __Church__ is located there today.

2. Which two rivers are located on both maps? __Delaware__ & __Schuylkill__

3. __Broad__ Street is also shown on both maps.

4. On the 1682 map, High Street appears to have been where __Market__ Street is today.

5. Examine the 1682 map. Find four small parks in the city. Circle them. Now find and circle the same four parks on today's map.

Cartographer's Name _____     Today's Date _____

---

Using COBBLESTONE as an
Integrated Reading Approach
All Issues
Blackline Master #1

Name _____

Date _____

## The Chautauqua Story

**Directions:** Answer the following questions in complete sentences.

1. Who were the two founders of Chautauqua?

   The two founders were Lewis Miller and John Vincent.

2. How did Edison's invention of the phonograph affect Chautauqua?

   It allowed people to listen to music in their homes rather than having to travel.

3. How did Chautauqua differ from other Sunday School institutions of its time?

   It was a combination of education, religion, recreation, and the arts.

4. Find and write a statement of evidence that supports the opinion that Mina Miller Edison was an active woman for her time.

   She ran two households (see p.17). / She was a volunteer for the Red Cross and a member of the DAR, the Missionary Services, the National Re-creation Association, and several art and music clubs (see p.18).

5. What changes took place in the latter 1800s that caused Mark Twain to call the years "The Gilded Age"?

   There was a shift from agriculture to in-dustry, and people moved from the farm to the city. The rich tried to imitate the British upper class.

6. Was "The Gilded Age" fair for all people? Explain your answer.

   Accept any reasonable answer.

Name _____

Date _____

# Map Interpretation

Route of the Transcontinental Railway

**Directions:** Use the map to answer the following questions about the route of the Transcontinental Railway.

1. List the five states through which the railway passed.

   1. _Nebraska_
   2. _Wyoming_
   3. _Utah_
   4. _Nevada_
   5. _California_

2. Which city was at the railway's western end? _Sacramento_

3. Which city was at the railway's eastern end? _Omaha_

4. Name two mountain ranges through which the railway passed.
   1. _Rocky Mountains_
   2. _Sierra Nevada_

5. How many miles was it from Omaha to Promontory Point? _About 1200 miles_

6. How many miles was it from Sacramento to Promontory Point? _About 700 miles_

7. Name two rivers the railway followed at different points.
   1. _Platte River_
   2. _Humboldt River_

8. How many tunnels were built? _Four_

---

Name _____

Date _____

# Sequencing a Story

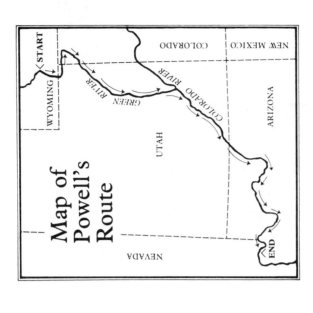

## Map of Powell's Route

**Directions:** The following events from the article "In Search of a River's End" are out of order. Place them in the correct sequence by numbering them from 1 to 6. The first one has been done for you.

_4_ A fire destroys the camp and injures some members of the expedition.

_6_ The expedition emerges without difficulty from the Grand Canyon.

_1_ John Powell and nine men move down the Green River toward the Colorado.

_3_ The "No-Name" strikes rocks and boulders and is broken in two.

_5_ Captain Howland and two others decide to quit the expedition and head out of the canyon.

_2_ The expedition quickly passes through Flaming Gorge on the river's fast current.

Identifying Reasons for Moving West
December 1980 Issue
Blackline Master #13

Name _____

Date _____

# Reasons for Moving West

**Directions:** Place an X through each statement below that identifies a reason why people moved west.

What would be your reason for going west?

*Accept any reasonable answer*

- I am a Mormon looking for religious freedom.
- I want to take advantage of the Homestead Act.
- I am going to take advantage of the modern conveniences.
- I am going because of the excellent climate.
- I want a fresh start after the Civil War.
- I want to settle in the dense forests of Nebraska.

---

Simulation: The Election of a President
October 1980 Issue
Blackline Master #11

Name _____

Date _____

# Simulation: The Election of a President

Political Party Key
N = Nationalists
C = Constitutional

**Presidential Election Returns** and **Electoral College Tally**

| States' Votes | SMITH N | JONES C | Elec. SMITH N | Elec. JONES C |
|---|---|---|---|---|
| Ala. 9 | 24% | 76% | | 9 |
| Alas. 3 | 43% | 57% | | 3 |
| Ariz. 6 | 62% | 38% | 6 | |
| Ark. 6 | 35% | 65% | | 6 |
| Calif. 45 | 51% | 49% | 45 | |
| Colo. 7 | 47% | 53% | | 7 |
| Conn. 8 | 45% | 55% | | 8 |
| Del. 3 | 61% | 39% | 3 | |
| D.C. 3 | 58% | 42% | 3 | |
| Fla. 17 | 53% | 47% | | 17 |
| Ga. 12 | 28% | 72% | | 12 |
| Haw. 4 | 52% | 48% | 4 | |
| Idaho 4 | 68% | 32% | 4 | |
| Ill. 26 | 41% | 59% | | 26 |
| Ind. 13 | 43% | 57% | | 13 |
| Iowa 8 | 59% | 41% | 8 | |
| Kan. 7 | 54% | 46% | 7 | |
| Ky. 9 | 40% | 60% | | 9 |
| La. 10 | 41% | 59% | | 10 |
| Me. 4 | 56% | 44% | 4 | |
| Md. 10 | 41% | 59% | | 10 |
| Mass. 14 | 39% | 61% | | 14 |
| Mich. 21 | 44% | 56% | | 21 |
| Minn. 10 | 53% | 47% | 10 | |
| Miss. 7 | 31% | 69% | | 7 |
| Mo. 12 | 58% | 42% | | 12 |
| Mont. 4 | 56% | 44% | 4 | |
| Nebr. 5 | 55% | 45% | 5 | |
| Nev. 3 | 63% | 37% | 3 | |
| N.H. 4 | 61% | 39% | 4 | |
| N.J. 17 | 41% | 59% | | 17 |
| N.M. 4 | 48% | 52% | | 4 |
| N.Y. 41 | 47% | 53% | | 41 |
| N.C. 13 | 38% | 62% | | 13 |
| N.D. 3 | 58% | 42% | 3 | |
| Ohio 25 | 47% | 53% | | 25 |
| Okla. 8 | 55% | 45% | 8 | |
| Ore. 6 | 65% | 35% | 6 | |
| Pa. 27 | 52% | 48% | 27 | |
| R.I. 4 | 47% | 53% | | 4 |
| S. Car. 8 | 40% | 60% | | 8 |
| S.D. 4 | 58% | 42% | 4 | |
| Tenn. 10 | 42% | 58% | | 10 |
| Texas 26 | 47% | 53% | | 26 |
| Utah 4 | 59% | 41% | 4 | |
| Vt. 3 | 56% | 44% | 3 | |
| Va. 12 | 47% | 53% | | 12 |
| Wash. 9 | 51% | 49% | 9 | |
| W. Va. 6 | 39% | 61% | | 6 |
| Wis. 11 | 48% | 52% | | 11 |
| Wyo. 3 | 54% | 46% | 3 | |
| **Total 538** | | | 206 | 332 |

82

## Follow the Drinking Gourd to Freedom

Filling in a Time Line
February 1981 Issue
Blackline Master #15

Name
Date

1492   1822   1830   1849   1863   1865   1859   1861

**Directions:** Cut out the events related to the history of slavery, and paste them next to their corresponding dates on the constellation time line.

|  |  |
| --- | --- |
| The Thirteenth Amendment abolishes all slavery. | 1865 |
| John Brown conducts a raid at Harper's Ferry to obtain guns for slaves to use in their fight for freedom. | 1859 |
| The Emancipation Proclamation is issued by President Lincoln. | 1863 |
| Harriet Tubman escapes to freedom. | 1849 |
| Thomas Garrett begins to help runaway slaves escape. | 1822 |
| The history of America's slavery begins when Columbus and his followers force natives to work. | 1492 |
| The words "Underground Railroad" are used for the first time to describe the way slaves escape to the North. | 1830 |
| The Civil War begins. | 1861 |

## In Search of Connecticut

In Search of Connecticut
January 1981 Issue
Blackline Master #14

Name
Date

```
W K T E P M B C H A R T E R
H A C H A R T F O R D G C S
A L G O N Q U I A N H S A T
L O C W I N T H R O P L V Q
E I P S M Z Y G J L U B E V
T A W O O D L A N D G K S T
```

**Directions:** Answer the questions below. Then find and circle the words in the above puzzle.

What is Connecticut's capital? HARTFORD

Connecticut has 275 of these, and spelunkers love to explore them. CAVES

What was the last name of the governor of the Connecticut Colony? WINTHROP

What was the last name of the person who said, "I only regret that I have but one life to lose for my country"? HALE

What was the last name of Connecticut's traitor? ARNOLD

What was the name of the Indians who lived in the forests of eastern America? WOODLAND

All of these Indians were part of which family? ALGONQUIAN

What document recognized the Colony of Connecticut and approved its self-government? CHARTER

# A Search-and-Find Mission

**Directions:** Use COBBLESTONE's June 1981 issue to find the answers to these questions:

1. What is the oldest navigational aid?

   _The lighthouse is the oldest navigational aid._

2. Where and when was America's first lighthouse built?

   _It was built in Boston in 1716._

3. What was the name of the first lightship?

   _The None was the first lightship._

4. Which lighthouse is located on the eastern shore of Lake Michigan?

   _Little Point Sable is located on the eastern shore._

5. Ida Lewis was the keeper of which lighthouse?

   _She was the keeper of Lime Rock._

6. What is the name of the British ship that Rebecca and Abigail Bates turned back from the shores of Scituate, Massachusetts?

   _The Hogue is the name of the ship._

7. Name two fuels that have been used to light a beacon.

   _wood, sperm whale oil,_
   _lard oil, kerosene,_
   _or electricity_

---

# Drawing Conclusions

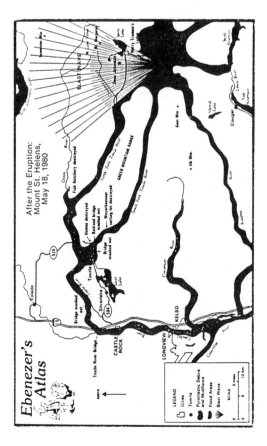

Ebenezer's Atlas

After the Eruption:
Mount St. Helens,
May 18, 1980

LEGEND
Cities
Towns
Pyroclastic Debris and Mudflows
Flood Areas
Blast Wave

SCALE
0    5    10 Km

**Directions:** Use the map to answer these questions:

1. Would you have had a flooding problem if you lived in Castle Rock? _Yes_

2. In which town might you have sought shelter if your home had been flooded?

   _Toledo, Silver Lake, or Cougar_

3. Whose home would you not want to have been visiting at the time of eruption?

   _Harry Truman's Lodge_

4. Could you drive from Toutle to Silverlake without a flooding problem? _No_

5. What problem would a train have encountered traveling northwest toward Toutle?

   _The railroad bridge was washed out._

83

## Revolutionary Inventions

**Directions:** Study the chart, then answer the questions below.

| Inventor | Invention | Date |
|---|---|---|
| Eli Whitney | Cotton Gin | 1793 |
| Robert Fulton | Steamboat | 1807 |
| Cyrus McCormick | Reaper | 1831 |
| Samuel Morse | Telegraph | 1837 |
| Elias Howe | Sewing Machine | 1846 |
| Alexander G. Bell | Telephone | 1876 |
| Thomas Edison | Light Bulb | 1879 |

1. Which invention most directly helped improve transportation?
   *The steamboat helped improve transportation.*

2. Which two inventions helped improve the textile industry?
   *The cotton gin and the sewing machine helped improve the textile industry.*

3. Which two inventions helped improve communications?
   *The telegraph and the telephone helped improve communications.*

4. Which invention helped improve farming?
   *The reaper helped improve farming.*

5. Which invention do *you* think brought about the greatest change? Explain your answer.
   *Accept any reasonable answer.*

---

## Get the Message?

**Directions:** The code Samuel Morse used to send messages on his telegraph is shown below. Use the code to discover the first message sent by the famous inventor.

```
A ·—        G ——·      L ·—··      Q ——·—     V ···—
B —···      H ····      M ——       R ·—·       W ·——
C —·—·      I ··        N —·        S ···       X —··—
D —··       J ·———      O ———       T —        Y —·——
E ·         K —·—       P ·——·      U ··—       Z ——··
F ··—·
```

·—— ···· ·—— ·—  —  —
 W    H   A   T

···  ·—  —  ····
 S   A   T   H

—·  ·—·  ——  —··
 G   O    D

·—  ·—·  ——  ··—  ——·  ····  —
 W   R    O   U   G    H    T  !

A Pictograph on World Wheat Production
April 1982 Issue
Blackline Master #25

Name _____

Date _____

# A Pictograph on World Wheat Production

## 1981-1982

| | |
|---|---|
| Soviet Union | 🌾🌾🌾🌾🌾🌾🌾 |
| United States | 🌾🌾🌾🌾🌾 |
| People's Republic of China | 🌾🌾🌾🌾 |
| India | 🌾🌾 |
| Canada | 🌾 |

KEY: 🌾 = ten million metric tons of wheat (rounded to the closest ten million)

**Directions:** Answer the following questions using the above graph:

1. What does each whole wheat symbol stand for? (How many tons does each represent?)
   Each symbol stands for 10 million tons of wheat.

2. By what number would you count to figure how many million metric tons of wheat each country produced?
   You would count by tens.

3. If a country produced exactly thirty million metric tons of wheat, how many wheat symbols would you draw?
   You would draw three symbols.

4. Which country produced the most wheat? Soviet Union

5. Which country produced the least wheat? Canada

---

Using the Prefix "Sub"
January 1982 Issue
Blackline Master #24

Name _____

Date _____

# Using the Prefix "Sub"

**Directions:** In the right-hand column are words that begin with the prefix "sub." In the left-hand column are the word meanings. Place the letter of the word in the space before its correct definition.

| | | | |
|---|---|---|---|
| R | 1. To give financial aid or assistance | A. | submarine |
| M | 2. Of lower order, rank, or importance | B. | sublet |
| J | 3. Below the earth's surface | C. | submerge |
| B | 4. To sublease to another | D. | subway |
| L | 5. Less important than the main topic | E. | subside |
| C | 6. To go down in the water | F. | subconscious |
| F | 7. Below the conscious level of the mind | G. | substandard |
| H | 8. On the edge of the tropics | H. | subversive |
| S | 9. Below normal | I. | subtropical |
| O | 10. Giving in to authority | J. | subterranean |
| A | 11. A ship that can operate above or below the water | K. | subhead |
| G | 12. Below an established standard | L. | subtopic |
| H | 13. Intending to destroy existing principles | M. | subordinate |
| K | 14. A heading or title below the main one | N. | subservient |
| N | 15. Helpful in an inferior way | O. | submission |
| D | 16. A railroad that goes underground | P. | subdivide |
| Q | 17. The outer part of a city | Q. | suburb |
| T | 18. Smaller than the main station | R. | subsidize |
| P | 19. To divide something into parts | S. | subnormal |
| E | 20. To fall, lower, or quiet down | T. | substation |

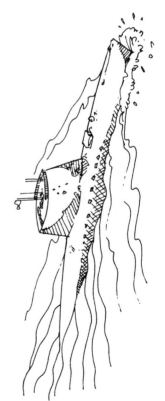

85

Drawing Different
Routes on a Map
June 1982 Issue
Blackline Master #27

Name _____

Date _____

# Early Fur Trade Routes

**Directions:** Below is a map showing the region where early fur traders hunted the beaver and other animals whose pelts were in demand. Follow the directions below the map to trace three possible routes used by the traders.

Possible Route #1: Using a red marker, make a dotted line starting at the northwest tip of Lake Winnipeg. Continue to the Sturgeon Weir River, go north to Reindeer Lake, Wallaston Lake, and Black Lake, and stop at Lake Athabasca.

Possible Route #2: Using a green marker, make a dotted line starting on the western edge of Lake Superior where the United States/Canadian border is shown. Continue to Rainy Lake, Lake of the Woods, and Lake Winnipeg. Then follow the Nelson River to Hudson Bay and rest.

Possible Route #3: Using a blue marker, make a dotted line starting at the point where the Saskatchewan River meets Lake Winnipeg. Follow the Saskatchewan River to the North Saskatchewan River, then continue to the Rocky Mountains. Stop and enjoy the view before you start trapping.

---

Using a Product Map
May 1982 Issue
Blackline Master #26

Name _____

Date _____

# Natural Resources of California

**Directions:** Use the product map of California (drawn in 1982) to answer questions about the state's natural resources.

CALIFORNIA'S NATURAL RESOURCES

1. Are forest products found mostly in the northern or southern portion of the state?

   _northern_

2. In which portion of the state are minerals primarily found?

   _Southern_

3. Are grapes grown near San Diego?

   _no_

4. Would you say that poultry products are a major source of income in this state?

   _no_

5. Do you think fruits are a major source of income for the state?

   _yes_

6. Is cotton widely grown in the state?

   _no_

7. Name the most abundant natural resource according to the map.

   _minerals_

8. Name the two resources that are the least abundant according to the map.

   _cotton_   _fish_

Medical Milestones
March 1983 Issue
Blackline Master #30

Name _____

Date _____

# Medical Milestones

**Directions:** In the box below are names of notable persons in medical history. Write the correct person's name on the line provided in the statement he or she would have made. (The March 1983 issue of COBBLESTONE will help you with this activity.)

| | | |
|---|---|---|
| Robert Koch | Sara Josephine Baker | John C. Warren |
| William Beaumont | Jonas Salk | |

1. "Observing the 'man with the window in his stomach' was remarkable," said _W. Beaumont_ in 1833. "I learned that the stomach does not grind or cook food, but instead gastric juices break it down in the digestive process."

2. "In 1955, I introduced a polio vaccine," said _Jonas Salk_.

3. "I remember when I used an anesthesia for the first time in surgery," said _John C. Warren_. "When the patient woke up after the operation, he told me he had felt no pain."

4. "I discovered that tuberculosis was not hereditary, but rather was caused by 'tubercle bacillus' and was passed into the air from infected lungs," said _Robert Koch_.

5. "I felt that through proper hygienic training, mothers and nurses could help prevent children from becoming ill," said _S. J. Baker_. "Back in 1908, it was difficult convincing city officials to adopt this concept of 'preventive medicine' to keep babies healthy."

---

Locating Countries
on a World Map
January 1983 Issue
Blackline Master #29

Name _____

Date _____

# Locating Countries on a World Map

**Directions:** Some countries of the world are shown below. Follow the directions at the bottom of the page to identify the home countries of some of our immigrants.

FRANCE 1. Use dark blue to color the country that gave us the Statue of Liberty.

JAPAN 2. Use green to color the country from which picture brides often came in the early 1900s.

GERMANY 3. Use red to color the home country of the Inspirationalists.

USSR 4. Use yellow to color the home country of many Jewish immigrants. It is the largest country in Europe and Asia.

CHINA 5. Use purple to color the home country of the immigrants who helped build our railroads.

A Visit to a
Shaker Community
April 1983 Issue
Blackline Master #31

## A Visit to a Shaker Community

**Directions:** Below is an imaginary letter written by a visitor to a Shaker community. Now that you are familiar with the lifestyle and beliefs of a Shaker, you will notice a problem with the letter. Some statements about Shakers are correct, and others are not. Draw a line through those statements about Shakers that are *not* correct.

Dear Ann,

I thought I would write to let you know how much I am enjoying my visit at the Shaker village. It has been a busy spring. Today I worked hard in Mary's garden. She has an especially lovely herb plot. Her husband, Mark, stayed inside to draft a political speech to support his candidate for Congress.

Benjamin has been busy making his slat-back chairs, and he has just completed a fine rocker with arms. You remember Frederick, don't you? Well, he has left to enlist in the military for two years. His cousin, Mark, is still tending the dairy herd. Martha has been her usual self, baking the best pies and breads for the community. By the way, Sara won the lottery and plans to build herself a fine mansion on the hill.

Well, it is time I join the rest of the community for dinner and scripture reading. I do hope this letter finds you well.

Sincerely,

Jane Owens

---

Unscrambling a Public Works Message
August 1983 Issue
Blackline Master #33

## Unscrambling a Public Works Message

**Directions:** Unscramble the letters to spell out words that are related to public works. Then unscramble the circled letters to answer the following question: What do you call manmade ducts that supply water to a community or city from a distance?

1. KSTARC    T R A C K S
2. IDBERG    B R I D G E
3. ESERW    S E W E R
4. VUIQRE    Q U I V E R
5. DMA    D A M
6. YSBAUW    S U B W A Y
7. ARWET    W A T E R
8. USB    B U S
9. TPSTNONARTRIAO    T R A N S P O R T A T I O N

1. What trains travel on.
2. A structure that is built across water or a road to allow passage.
3. An underground drain to carry waste and water.
4. Something you might do if you walked on a suspension bridge.
5. A structure that holds back water.
6. An underground railroad.
7. A natural resource we need to survive.
8. One form of public transportation that moves several people at a time.
9. The business of moving passengers or goods from one place to another.

Put the circled letters here: C D S Q A V E U I

Now unscramble them to answer the above question: A Q U E D U C T S

A Jazzy Crossword Puzzle
October 1983 Issue
Blackline Master #34

Name _____

Date _____

# A Jazzy Crossword Puzzle

**Directions:** Test your knowledge of jazz in this puzzle. The clues are below.

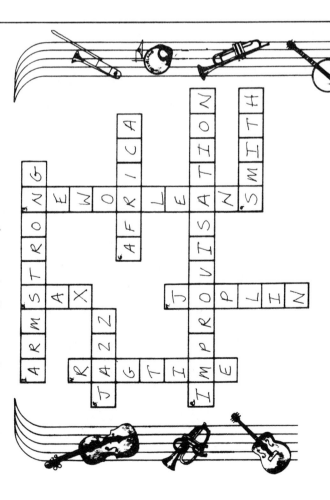

**Across**

1. The last name of a famous jazz trumpet player.

5. A lively, rhythmical form of music.

6. The rhythms of jazz have their roots here.

8. The act of changing and experimenting with music as it is played.

9. The last name of a famous blues singer.

**Down**

2. The first syllable of this brass wind instrument is its inventor's last name.

3. This city is known as the "cradle of jazz."

4. It is characterized by jerky rhythms in its tunes.

7. He was "King of Ragtime."

---

Finding the Key Word
November 1983 Issue
Blackline Master #35

Name _____

Date _____

# Finding the Key Word

**Directions:** Below is a list of questions. Underline the key word you would use to look up the answers in an encyclopedia or a book index.

1. When was the telegraph invented?

2. What city is the capital of Utah?

3. What is the diet of a caribou?

4. What is the Thirteenth Amendment to the Constitution?

5. What language is spoken in Brazil?

6. Was Thomas Jefferson in favor of a strong central government?

7. What is the climate of Greece?

8. How many moons orbit the planet of Jupiter?

9. Which country produces the most wheat in the world?

10. How does a telephone work?

11. What type of instrument did Louis Armstrong play?

12. Where was America's first lighthouse built?

13. What is the oldest building in America?

14. When did the Mayflower sail to America?

15. How did Patrick Henry feel about writing a constitution?

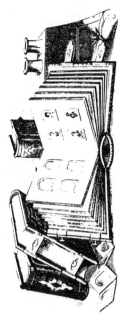

A Bar Graph
June 1984 Issue
Blackline Master #38

Name _____

Date _____

# A Bar Graph: Which Program Would Help You?

**Directions:** Students were questioned to see which type of academic computer program would help them in a particular subject. The results are shown in the box. Below the box are questions for you to answer. Then make a bar graph using the information about which computer programs were needed.

| | |
|---|---|
| Spelling | 卌 ||| |
| Math Facts | 卌 卌 || |
| State Capitals | 卌 |
| Word Definitions | ||| |
| Our Solar System | || |

1. How many students wanted a math facts program? _12_

2. How many wanted one on the solar system? _2_

3. How many more wanted state capitals than word definitions? _2_

Computer Programs Needed by Students

```
16 |
14 |
12 |
10 |
 8 |
 6 |
 4 |
 2 |
 0 |_____
    Spelling  Math    State     Word      Solar
              Facts   Capitals  Definitions System
```

Number of Students Responding

---

How Well Did You Listen?
December 1983 Issue
Blackline Master #36

Name _____

Date _____

# How Well Did You Listen?

**Directions:** This is a listening test. Someone will read the article "Living in the Dust Bowl." The questions and answers below will also be read once to you. Circle the letter of the correct answer.

1. In which decade did the Dust Bowl occur?

   A. 1920s
   B. 1930s
   C. 1940s
   D. 1950s

2. A "black blizzard" was a wall of flying:

   A. insects
   B. mud
   C. soil
   D. soot

3. Which of these was mentioned as a problem for Great Plains farmers?

   A. poor fertilizer
   B. acid soil
   C. locust plague
   D. windstorms

4. A native of North Dakota recalled that by noon each day the sky was:

   A. pale yellow
   B. slightly pink
   C. grayish
   D. black

5. Only one of these was mentioned as a problem homeowners faced. Which was it?

   A. The houses needed painting.
   B. Dust covered everything in the home.
   C. Dust clogged the chimneys.
   D. The sidewalks cracked.

6. According to the article, which of these activities continued during the Dust Bowl?

   A. harvest festivals
   B. planting of crops
   C. football tournaments
   D. fund-raising events

90

Name _____

Date _____

# The Chautauqua Story

**Directions:** Answer the following questions in complete sentences.

1. Who were the two founders of Chautauqua?

_____

_____

2. How did Edison's invention of the phonograph affect Chautauqua?

_____

_____

3. How did Chautauqua differ from other Sunday School institutions of its time?

_____

_____

4. Find and write a statement of evidence that supports the opinion that Mina Miller Edison was an active woman for her time.

_____

_____

_____

5. What changes took place in the latter 1800s that caused Mark Twain to call the years "The Gilded Age"?

_____

_____

_____

6. Was "The Gilded Age" fair for all people? Explain your answer.

_____

_____

_____

Name _____

Date _____

# Notable Person Reference List

*These people are prominently featured in the appropriate issue. More people can be found in the COBBLESTONE Index.*

| | | | |
|---|---|---|---|
| January 1980 | George Washington | March 1982 | Santa Anna<br>Davy Crockett |
| February 1980 | Thomas Edison | April 1982 | Cyrus McCormick |
| March 1980 | John Adams<br>Sam Adams<br>Crispus Attucks<br>Peter Faneuil<br>Paul Revere | June 1982 | LaSalle |
| | | August 1982 | P. T. Barnum<br>Ringling Brothers<br>William Saroyan<br>Tom Thumb |
| April 1980 | John James Audubon | | |
| May 1980 | Casey Jones | October 1982 | Canvas White |
| June 1980 | John Wesley Powell | November 1982 | Frederic Remington |
| July 1980 | Milton Bradley<br>George Parker | December 1982 | Jacob Riis |
| August 1980 | George Carmack<br>Jack London | February 1983 | Shirley Chisholm<br>Martin Luther King, Jr.<br>Malcolm X<br>Nat Turner |
| September 1980 | William Clark<br>Thomas Jefferson<br>Meriwether Lewis<br>Sacajawea<br>York | March 1983 | Dr. Sara Josephine Baker<br>Cotton Mather |
| | | April 1983 | Ann Lee |
| October 1980 | Carrie Chapman Catt<br>Thomas Nast<br>Victoria C. Woodhull | May 1983 | Louis Braille<br>Helen Keller<br>Anne Sullivan |
| November 1980 | Deborah Sampson | June 1983 | Adolph Bandelier<br>Alfred Kidder |
| December 1980 | Willa Cather<br>Red Cloud | September 1983 | Haym Salomon |
| January 1981 | Benedict Arnold<br>Nathan Hale | October 1983 | Eubie Blake<br>Scott Joplin<br>Bessie Smith |
| February 1981 | John Brown<br>Thomas Garrett<br>Harriet Tubman | November 1983 | Andrew Carnegie<br>Melvil Dewey<br>Anne Carroll Moore |
| March 1981 | Cabeza de Vaca<br>Coronado<br>Juan de Onate | January 1984 | Robert Goddard |
| | | February 1984 | Will Rogers<br>Sequoya |
| April 1981 | Mary Ann Bickerdyke<br>Matthew Brady<br>Ross Greenhow<br>Thaddeus Lowe | May 1984 | Mark Twain |
| | | June 1984 | Charles Babbage |
| May 1981 | Harry Truman of<br>Mount St. Helens | July 1984 | Mina Miller Edison<br>Lewis Miller<br>John Heyl Vincent |
| June 1981 | Ida Lewis | | |
| July 1981 | Eugene Carnan<br>Valentina Tereshkova | August 1984 | Avery Brundage<br>Babe Didrikson<br>Jesse Owens |
| August 1981 | Buffalo Bill | September 1984 | Alexander Hamilton<br>Charles Willson Peale<br>Noah Webster<br>Phillis Wheatley |
| September 1981 | Andrew Carnegie<br>Elijah McCoy | | |
| October 1981 | Samuel B. Morse | October 1984 | Leif Eiriksson |
| November 1981 | Horace Mann | | |
| December 1981 | Marcus Whitman | November 1984 | Margaret Chase Smith |
| January 1982 | Jacques-Yves Cousteau | December 1984 | Samuel Pierpont Langley<br>Orville & Wilbur Wright |
| February 1982 | Harriet Beecher Stowe | | |

# COBBLESTONE Trivia

| CANALERS | JOHNNYCAKES | ATHLON |
|---|---|---|
| October 1982   p. 22 | September 1983   p.41 | August 1984   p. 10 |
| THE BRONCO BUSTER November 1982   p. 8 | CAJUN October 1983   p. 34 | BLUE-BACKED SPELLER September 1984   p. 11 |
| STREET ARABS December 1982   p. 20 | MESOPOTAMIA November 1983   p. 37 | KENSINGTON STONE October 1984   p. 21 |
| XENOPHOBIA January 1983   p. 33 | PROTOZOA December 1983   p.12 | FILIBUSTER November 1984   p. 29 |
| BLACK CODES February 1983   p. 17 | EPCOT January 1984   p. 30 | HINDENBURG December 1984   p. 34 |
| QUACK March 1983   p. 15 | MAIZE February 1984   p. 19 | |
| UTOPIA April 1983   p. 18 | NEW DEAL March 1984   p. 35 | |
| PUBLIC LAW 94-142 May 1983   p. 35 | CHANTEY April 1984   p. 15 | |
| CARBON-14 June 1983   p. 15 | CLERMONT May 1984   p. 20 | |
| FOLKLORE July 1983   p. 22 | ABACUS June 1984   p. 6 | |
| PUBLIC WORKS August 1983   p. 4 | MUCKRAKER July 1984   p. 24 | |

| CALLITHUMPIAN BAND | SODDIE | PAPYRUS |
|---|---|---|
| January 1980   p. 6 | December 1980   p. 32 | November 1981   p. 9 |
| BETTY LAMP February 1980   p. 8 | SACHEM January 1981   p. 11 | INDEPENDENCE ROCK December 1981   p. 20 |
| "THE GRASSHOPPER" March 1980   p. 38 | DRINKING GOURD February 1981   p. 38 | TURTLE January 1982   p. 10 |
| TAXIDERMY April 1980   p. 44 | COPERNICUS March 1981   p. 37 | LOOKING GLASS February 1982   p. 27 |
| MULLIGAN May 1980   p. 38 | APPOMATTOX April 1981   p. 7 | BOWIE KNIFE March 1982   p. 17 |
| HAVASUPAI June 1980   p. 7 | RING OF FIRE May 1981   p. 5 | GREEN REVOLUTION April 1982   p. 12 |
| MORRIS July 1980   p. 9 | NANTUCKET June 1981   p. 28 | THE COUNT OF MONTE CRISTO May 1982   p. 24 |
| SOURDOUGHS August 1980   p. 20 | YURI GAGARIN July 1981   p. 40 | RENDEZVOUS June 1982   p. 15 |
| MONTICELLO September 1980   p. 23 | CLOVEN August 1981   p. 31 | REMUDA July 1982   p. 13 |
| TEDDY BEARS October 1980   p. 36 | BREAD COLONIES September 1981   p. 17 | HIPPODROME August 1982   p. 13 |
| SANDWICH November 1980   p. 26 | OVERLAND ROUTE October 1981   p. 4 | ERA September 1982   p. 20 |

Name _____

Date _____

# Notable Person Activity: Research Sheet

Notable Person: _____

Resource: Title: _____

Publisher: _____

Copyright Date: _____

Page Number: _____

When did the person live? _____

Where did the person live? _____

Why is the person famous? _____

_____

_____

What was the person's contribution to history? _____

_____

_____

What was most interesting to you about the person? _____

_____

_____

When and how did the person die? _____

_____

_____

Other notes: _____

_____

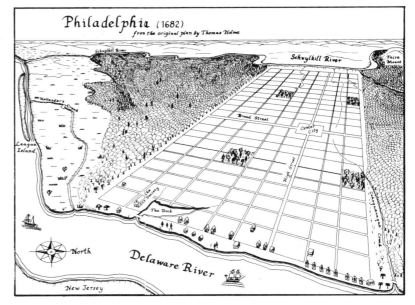

# Then & Now:
# Comparing Maps
# of the Same Area

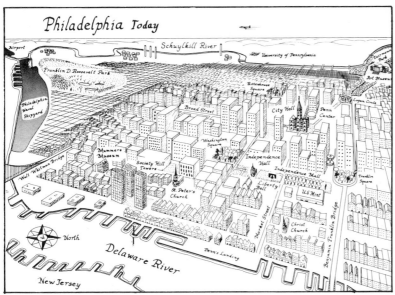

**Directions:** Fill in the blanks.

1. Find "Center City" on the 1682 map. A _____ is located there today.

2. Which two rivers are located on both maps? _____ &

   _____ .

3. _____ Street is also shown on both maps.

4. On the 1682 map, High Street appears to have been where _____ Street is

   today.

5. Examine the 1682 map. Find four small parks in the city. Circle them. Now find and circle the
   same four parks on today's map.

Cartographer's Name _____     Today's Date _____

# Applying for a Patent

**Directions:** Draw a design of your invention. Then fill out the patent application form below.

Patent Application

Inventor's Name: _____

                           Last                       First           Middle I.

Address: _____

        Street

_____

City or Town          State          Zip

Telephone: _____

        Area Code           Number

Description of Invention: (Please print clearly.)

_____

_____

_____

_____

_____

Draw a picture of your invention in the space below:

Name of Invention: _____

# Writing a Newspaper Story

**Directions:** Write your own eyewitness account of the Boston Massacre. Then draw a picture of the incident in the space provided.

*Boston Star*

No. 8                                        March 6, 1770

★★★★★★★★★★★★★★★★★★★★★★★★★★★★★★★★★★★★

FIVE CITIZENS KILLED!

by _____
   *Boston Star* Staff

_____

_____

_____

_____

_____

_____

_____

_____

_____

_____

_____                    Photograph: _____

_____

_____

_____

_____

_____

Name _____

Date _____

# Map Interpretation

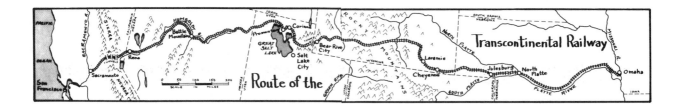

**Directions:**  Use the map to answer the following questions about the route of the Transcontinental Railway.

1.  List the five states through which the railway passed.

    1. _____      4. _____

    2. _____      5. _____

    3. _____

2.  Which city was at the railway's western end? _____

3.  Which city was at the railway's eastern end? _____

4.  Name two mountain ranges through which the railway passed.

    1. _____      2. _____

5.  How many miles was it from Omaha to Promontory Point? _____

6.  How many miles was it from Sacramento to Promontory Point? _____

7.  Name two rivers the railway followed at different points.

    1. _____      2. _____

8.  How many tunnels were built? _____

Name _____

Date _____

# Sequencing a Story

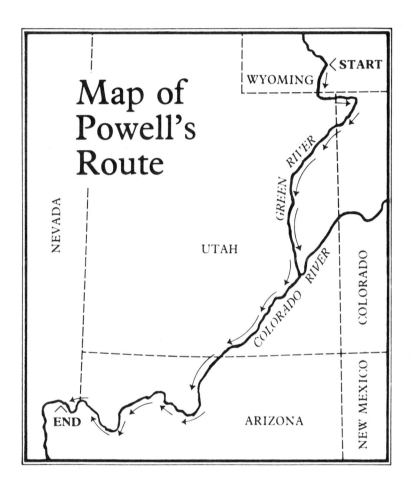

**Directions:** The following events from the article "In Search of a River's End" are out of order. Place them in the correct sequence by numbering them from 1 to 6. The first one has been done for you.

_____ A fire destroys the camp and injures some members of the expedition.

_____ The expedition emerges without difficulty from the Grand Canyon.

____1____ John Powell and nine men move down the Green River toward the Colorado.

_____ The "No-Name" strikes rocks and boulders and is broken in two.

_____ Captain Howland and two others decide to quit the expedition and head out of the canyon.

_____ The expedition quickly passes through Flaming Gorge on the river's fast current.

Prospector's Name _____

Today's Date _____

# How to Pan for Gold

**Directions:** After reading the article "Panning for Gold," use the lines below to explain in your own words how it is done.

_____

_____

_____

_____

_____

_____

_____

_____

_____

_____

_____

_____

_____

_____

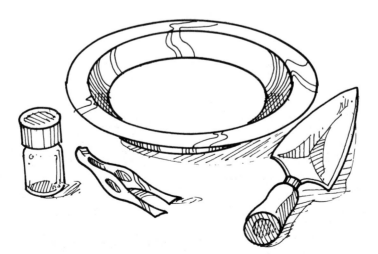

Name _____

Date _____

# Simulation: The Election of a President

Political Party Key
  N = Nationalists
  C = Constitutional

**Presidential Election Returns**

| States' Votes | SMITH N | JONES C |
|---|---|---|
| Ala. | 24% | 76% |
| Alas. | 43% | 57% |
| Ariz. | 62% | 38% |
| Ark. | 35% | 65% |
| Calif. | 51% | 49% |
| Colo. | 47% | 53% |
| Conn. | 45% | 55% |
| Del. | 61% | 39% |
| D.C. | 58% | 42% |
| Fla. | 53% | 47% |
| Ga. | 28% | 72% |
| Haw. | 52% | 48% |
| Idaho | 68% | 32% |
| Ill. | 41% | 59% |
| Ind. | 43% | 57% |
| Iowa | 59% | 41% |
| Kan. | 54% | 46% |
| Ky. | 40% | 60% |
| La. | 41% | 59% |
| Me. | 56% | 44% |
| Md. | 41% | 59% |
| Mass. | 39% | 61% |
| Mich. | 44% | 56% |
| Minn. | 53% | 47% |
| Miss. | 31% | 69% |
| Mo. | 58% | 42% |
| Mont. | 56% | 44% |
| Nebr. | 55% | 45% |
| Nev. | 63% | 37% |
| N.H. | 61% | 39% |
| N.J. | 41% | 59% |
| N.M. | 48% | 52% |
| N.Y. | 47% | 53% |
| N.C. | 38% | 62% |
| N.D. | 58% | 42% |
| Ohio | 47% | 53% |
| Okla. | 55% | 45% |
| Ore. | 65% | 35% |
| Pa. | 52% | 48% |
| R.I. | 47% | 53% |
| S. Car. | 40% | 60% |
| S.D. | 58% | 42% |
| Tenn. | 42% | 58% |
| Texas | 47% | 53% |
| Utah | 59% | 41% |
| Vt. | 56% | 44% |
| Va. | 47% | 53% |
| Wash. | 51% | 49% |
| W. Va. | 39% | 61% |
| Wis. | 48% | 52% |
| Wyo. | 54% | 46% |

**Electoral College Tally**

| States' Votes | SMITH N | JONES C |
|---|---|---|
| Ala. 9 | | |
| Alas. 3 | | |
| Ariz. 6 | | |
| Ark. 6 | | |
| Calif. 45 | | |
| Colo. 7 | | |
| Conn. 8 | | |
| Del. 3 | | |
| D.C. 3 | | |
| Fla. 17 | | |
| Ga. 12 | | |
| Haw. 4 | | |
| Idaho 4 | | |
| Ill. 26 | | |
| Ind. 13 | | |
| Iowa 8 | | |
| Kan. 7 | | |
| Ky. 9 | | |
| La. 10 | | |
| Me. 4 | | |
| Md. 10 | | |
| Mass. 14 | | |
| Mich. 21 | | |
| Minn. 10 | | |
| Miss. 7 | | |
| Mo. 12 | | |
| Mont. 4 | | |
| Nebr. 5 | | |
| Nev. 3 | | |
| N.H. 4 | | |
| N.J. 17 | | |
| N.M. 4 | | |
| N.Y. 41 | | |
| N.C. 13 | | |
| N.D. 3 | | |
| Ohio 25 | | |
| Okla. 8 | | |
| Ore. 6 | | |
| Pa. 27 | | |
| R.I. 4 | | |
| S. Car. 8 | | |
| S.D. 4 | | |
| Tenn. 10 | | |
| Texas 26 | | |
| Utah 4 | | |
| Vt. 3 | | |
| Va. 12 | | |
| Wash. 9 | | |
| W. Va. 6 | | |
| Wis. 11 | | |
| Wyo. 3 | | |
| **Total 538** | | |
| Majority 270 | | |

Drawing a Family Tree
November 1980 Issue
Blackline Master #12

Name _____

Date _____

# Drawing a Family Tree

**Directions:** Take the "family tree" home and fill it in as much as possible.

_____ (your name)

_____ (date of birth)

_____ (place of birth)

(mother)                    (father)

_____        _____

_____        _____

_____        _____

(grandmother)    (grandfather)    (grandmother)    (grandfather)

_____  _____  _____  _____

_____  _____  _____  _____

_____  _____  _____  _____

Name _____

Date _____

# Reasons for Moving West

**Directions:** Place an X through each statement below that identifies a reason why people moved west.

What would be your reason for going west?

I am a Mormon looking for religious freedom.

I am going because of the excellent climate.

I want to take advantage of the Homestead Act.

I am going to take advantage of the modern conveniences.

I want a fresh start after the Civil War.

I want to settle in the dense forests of Nebraska.

Name _____

Date _____

# In Search of Connecticut

```
W  K  T  E  P  M  B  C  H  A  R  T  E  R
H  A  C  H  A  R  T  F  O  R  D  G  C  S
A  L  G  O  N  Q  U  I  A  N  H  S  A  T
L  O  C  W  I  N  T  H  R  O  P  L  V  Q
E  I  P  S  M  Z  Y  G  J  L  U  B  E  V
T  A  W  O  O  D  L  A  N  D  G  K  S  T
```

**Directions:** Answer the questions below. Then find and circle the words in the above puzzle.

What is Connecticut's capital?                                   _ _ _ _ _ _ _ _

Connecticut has 275 of these, and spelunkers love to explore them.                                                _ _ _ _ _ _

What was the last name of the governor of the Connecticut Colony?                                              _ _ _ _ _ _ _ _ _

What was the last name of the person who said, "I only regret that I have but one life to lose for my country"?      _ _ _ _ _

What was the last name of Connecticut's traitor?                _ _ _ _ _ _ _

What was the name of the Indians who lived in the forests of eastern America?                                _ _ _ _ _ _ _ _

All of these Indians were part of which family?                 _ _ _ _ _ _ _ _ _ _

What document recognized the Colony of Connecticut and approved its self-government?                             _ _ _ _ _ _ _

# Follow the Drinking Gourd to Freedom

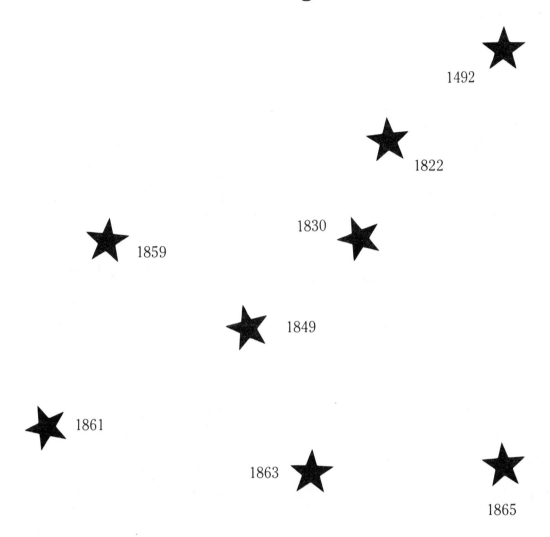

1492

1822

1830

1859

1849

1861

1863

1865

**Directions:** Cut out the events related to the history of slavery, and paste them next to their corresponding dates on the constellation time line.

| | |
|---|---|
| The Thirteenth Amendment abolishes all slavery. | Thomas Garrett begins to help runaway slaves escape. |
| John Brown conducts a raid at Harper's Ferry to obtain guns for slaves to use in their fight for freedom. | The history of America's slavery begins when Columbus and his followers force natives to work. |
| The Emancipation Proclamation is issued by President Lincoln. | The words "Underground Railroad" are used for the first time to describe the way slaves escape to the North. |
| Harriet Tubman escapes to freedom. | The Civil War begins. |

Name _____

Date _____

# Civil War Uniforms

**Directions:** Examples of uniforms worn by Confederate and Union infantrymen are shown below. Use the chart to color them properly.

| Union Infantryman | Color | Confederate Infantryman |
|---|---|---|
| musket stock & sling | brown | jacket, pants, shoes, rifle stock, & canteen |
| wool flannel shirt | gray | hat, blanket roll |
| tin cup, bayonet, musket lock, barrel, & fittings | silver | drinking cup, bayonet, rifle lock, barrel, & fittings |
| waist belt, haversack, cap visor | black | |
| | white | haversack |
| buttons | yellow | bayonet scabbard tip |
| sack coat, forage cap | dark blue | |
| pants | sky blue | |

Volcanologist's Name _____

Today's Date _____

# Drawing Conclusions

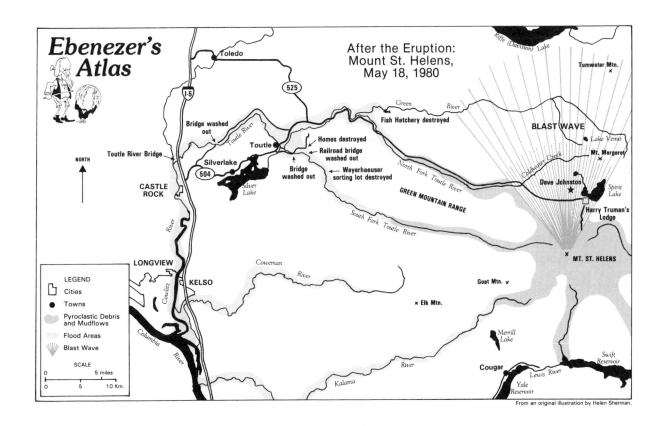

From an original illustration by Helen Sherman.

**Directions:** Use the map to answer these questions:

1. Would you have had a flooding problem if you lived in Castle Rock? _____

2. In which town might you have sought shelter if your home had been flooded?

   _____

3. Whose home would you not want to have been visiting at the time of eruption?

   _____

4. Could you drive from Toutle to Silverlake without a flooding problem? _____

5. What problem would a train have encountered traveling northwest toward Toutle?

   _____

Name _____

Date _____

# A Search-and-Find Mission

**Directions:** Use COBBLESTONE's June 1981 issue to find the answers to these questions:

1. What is the oldest navigational aid?

_____

2. Where and when was America's first lighthouse built?

_____

3. What was the name of the first lightship?

_____

4. Which lighthouse is located on the eastern shore of Lake Michigan?

_____

5. Ida Lewis was the keeper of which lighthouse?

_____

6. What is the name of the British ship that Rebecca and Abigail Bates turned back from the shores of Scituate, Massachusetts?

_____

7. Name two fuels that have been used to light a beacon.

_____

_____

_____

_____

# A Voyage to the Moon

**Directions:** Imagine that NASA is taking applications for the first students to go the moon. Think over why you think you should be accepted, then fill out the form below.

Application for a Voyage to the Moon

Name: _____ Sex: _____

         Last        First        Middle I.

Address: _____ Age: _____

         Street

         _____

         City or Town      State      Zip

Telephone: _____

         Area Code        Number

Birth Date: _____

         Month        Day       Year

General Health: _____

Hobbies: _____

Please answer the following questions in complete sentences:

Why do you think you should be selected as one of the first students to go to the moon?

_____

_____

_____

How would you share your experience when you returned from the voyage?

_____

_____

The Indian and the Buffalo
August 1981 Issue
Blackline Master #20

Drawn by _____

Date _____

# The Indians' Many Uses of the Buffalo

**Directions:** Think over the different ways Indians used the buffalo. Draw a picture in the space below that shows at least three things Indians made from parts of a buffalo.

Name _____

Date _____

# Revolutionary Inventions

**Directions:**  Study the chart, then answer the questions below.

| Inventor | Invention | Date |
|----------|-----------|------|
| Eli Whitney | Cotton Gin | 1793 |
| Robert Fulton | Steamboat | 1807 |
| Cyrus McCormick | Reaper | 1831 |
| Samuel Morse | Telegraph | 1837 |
| Elias Howe | Sewing Machine | 1846 |
| Alexander G. Bell | Telephone | 1876 |
| Thomas Edison | Light Bulb | 1879 |

1.  Which invention most directly helped improve transportation?

_____

2.  Which two inventions helped improve the textile industry?

_____

3.  Which two inventions helped improve communications?

_____

4.  Which invention helped improve farming?

_____

5.  Which invention do *you* think brought about the greatest change? Explain your answer.

_____

_____

_____

# Get the Message?

**Directions:** The code Samuel Morse used to send messages on his telegraph is shown below. Use the code to discover the first message sent by the famous inventor.

| | | | | | | | | | |
|---|---|---|---|---|---|---|---|---|---|
| A | •- | G | --• | L | — | Q | ••-• | V | •••- |
| B | -••• | H | •••• | M | -- | R | •-• | W | •-- |
| C | -•-• | I | •• | N | -• | S | ••• | X | -••- |
| D | -•• | J | •--- | O | --- | T | - | Y | -•-- |
| E | • | K | -•- | P | •--• | U | ••- | Z | --•• |
| F | ••-• | | | | | | | | |

•--　•••• 　•-　-
____　____　____　____

••••　•-　-　••••
____　____　____　____

--•　---　-••
____　____　____

•--　•-•　••　---　--•　••••　-
____　____　____　____　____　____　____ !

What Does Not Belong?
November 1981 Issue
Blackline Master #23

Name _____

Date _____

# What Does Not Belong?

**Directions:**

1. Draw a picture of how a schoolroom might have looked in the 1800s. Include five items from our present time period that do not belong in the picture.

2. Trade your picture with another student. Circle the items that do not belong in the old-time schoolroom.

Name _____

Date _____

# Using the Prefix "Sub"

**Directions:** In the right-hand column are words that begin with the prefix "sub." In the left-hand column are the word meanings. Place the letter of the word in the space before its correct definition.

1. _____  To give financial aid or assistance                A.  submarine

2. _____  Of lower order, rank, or importance               B.  sublet

3. _____  Below the earth's surface                          C.  submerge

4. _____  To sublease to another                             D.  subway

5. _____  Less important than the main topic                E.  subside

6. _____  To go down in the water                            F.  subconscious

7. _____  Below the conscious level of the mind             G.  substandard

8. _____  On the edge of the tropics                         H.  subversive

9. _____  Below normal                                       I.  subtropical

10. _____  Giving in to authority                            J.  subterranean

11. _____  A ship that can operate above or below            K.  subhead
             the water

12. _____  Below an established standard                     L.  subtopic

13. _____  Intending to destroy existing principles          M.  subordinate

14. _____  A heading or title below the main one             N.  subservient

15. _____  Helpful in an inferior way                        O.  submission

16. _____  A railroad that goes underground                  P.  subdivide

17. _____  The outer part of a city                          Q.  suburb

18. _____  Smaller than the main station                     R.  subsidize

19. _____  To divide something into parts                    S.  subnormal

20. _____  To fall, lower, or quiet down                     T.  substation

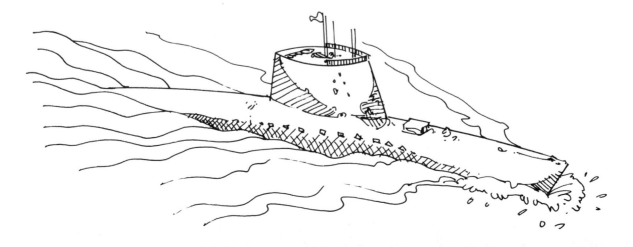

Name _____

Date _____

# A Pictograph on World Wheat Production

# 1981–1982

| Soviet Union | 🌾 🌾 🌾 🌾 🌾 🌾 🌾 🌾 🌾 |
| United States | 🌾 🌾 🌾 🌾 🌾 🌾 🌾 🌾 |
| People's Republic of China | 🌾 🌾 🌾 🌾 🌾 🌾 |
| India | 🌾 🌾 🌾 🌾 |
| Canada | 🌾 🌾 |

KEY: 🌾 = ten million metric tons of wheat (rounded to the closest ten million)

**Directions:** Answer the following questions using the above graph:

1. What does each whole wheat symbol stand for? (How many tons does each represent?)

_____

2. By what number would you count to figure how many million metric tons of wheat each country produced?

_____

3. If a country produced exactly thirty million metric tons of wheat, how many wheat symbols would you draw?

_____

4. Which country produced the most wheat? _____

5. Which country produced the least wheat? _____

Name _____

Date _____

# Natural Resources of California

**Directions:** Use the product map of California (drawn in 1982) to answer questions about the state's natural resources.

1. Are forest products found mostly in the northern or southern portion of the state?

   _____

2. In which portion of the state are minerals primarily found?

   _____

3. Are grapes grown near San Diego?

   _____

4. Would you say that poultry products are a major source of income in this state?

   _____

5. Do you think fruits are a major source of income for the state?

   _____

6. Is cotton widely grown in the state?

   _____

7. Name the most abundant natural resource according to the map.

   _____

8. Name the two resources that are the least abundant according to the map.

   _____    _____

CALIFORNIA'S NATURAL RESOURCES

△ FRUIT
▲ GRAPES
◆ VEGETABLES
✱ POULTRY
◇ FISH
✧ DAIRY PRODUCTS
◆ CATTLE
◖ COTTON

● FOREST PRODUCTS
☆ NATURAL GAS
★ OIL
○ MINERALS

Name _____

Date _____

# Early Fur Trade Routes

**Directions:** Below is a map showing the region where early fur traders hunted the beaver and other animals whose pelts were in demand. Follow the directions below the map to trace three possible routes used by the traders.

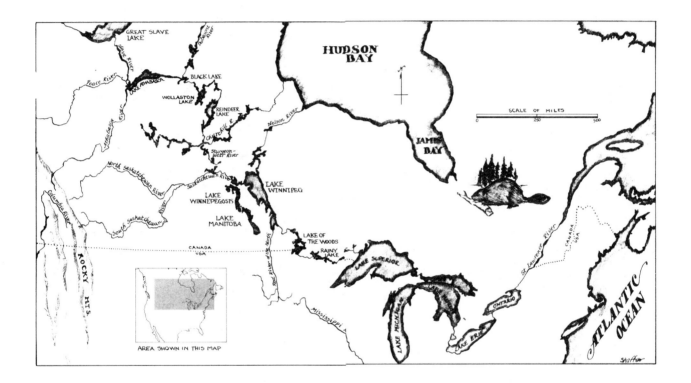

Possible Route #1:   Using a red marker, make a dotted line starting at the northwest tip of Lake Winnipeg. Continue to the Sturgeon Weir River, go north to Reindeer Lake, Wallaston Lake, and Black Lake, and stop at Lake Athabasca.

Possible Route #2:   Using a green marker, make a dotted line starting on the western edge of Lake Superior where the United States/Canadian border is shown. Continue to Rainy Lake, Lake of the Woods, and Lake Winnipeg. Then follow the Nelson River to Hudson Bay and rest.

Possible Route #3:   Using a blue marker, make a dotted line starting at the point where the Saskatchewan River meets Lake Winnipeg. Follow the Saskatchewan River to the North Saskatchewan River, then continue to the Rocky Mountains. Stop and enjoy the view before you start trapping.

Name _____

Date _____

# Designing Your Own Brand

**Directions:** Guess the names of the brands in the chart below.

### How to Read a Brand

Hundreds of different brands traveled over western soil on the hides of cattle and horses. A cowboy had to be an expert at reading these brands. He knew many brands from memory and knew how to read any brand he didn't recognize. Here are some tips to help you read brands.

Brands are usually read from top to bottom, left to right. Horizontal lines are read as bars. Diagonal lines are read as slashes. Example:

T̄ is the Bar T Brand.

—/ is the Bar Slash Brand.

Symbols that sit on curved lines rock. Symbols attached to the bottoms of curves swing. Example:

ℛ is the Rocking R Brand.

6 is the Swinging Six Brand.

Symbols can be boxed or circled. Example:

[B] is the Box B Brand.

Ⓒ is the Circle C Brand.

Letters are lazy if they lie on their sides. Letters tumble if they look like they're about to fall. Example:

Ƹ is the Lazy M Brand.

⅄ is the Tumbling T Brand.

Brands sometimes use parts of circles. Example:

Â is the Quarter Circle A Brand.

Brand symbols can do just about anything! Example:

Ƹ is the Walking F Brand.

NAME THAT BRAND

**Brands answers**

| | | |
|---|---|---|
| 1. B Quarter Circle | 8. Bar T | 15. Swinging H |
| 2. Running D | 9. Walking Y | 16. Lazy 2 |
| 3. Me Too | 10. Box R | 17. Rocking K |
| 4. Lazy E | 11. Rocking Chair | 18. Lazy 5 |
| 5. Bar BQ | 12. Slash A | 19. Flying U |
| 6. Quarter Circle O Bar | 13. Quarter Circle O | 20. Circle K |
| 7. Swinging V | 14. Quarter Circle V Bar | |

Design your own brand in this space, then write its name on the back of this paper.

Name _____

Date _____

# Locating Countries on a World Map

**Directions:** Some countries of the world are shown below. Follow the directions at the bottom of the page to identify the home countries of some of our immigrants.

1. Use dark blue to color the country that gave us the Statue of Liberty.

2. Use green to color the country from which picture brides often came in the early 1900s.

3. Use red to color the home country of the Inspirationalists.

4. Use yellow to color the home country of many Jewish immigrants. It is the largest country in Europe and Asia.

5. Use purple to color the home country of the immigrants who helped build our railroads.

Name _____

Date _____

# Medical Milestones

**Directions:** In the box below are names of notable persons in medical history. Write the correct person's name on the line provided in the statement he or she would have made. (The March 1983 issue of COBBLESTONE will help you with this activity.)

---

**Robert Koch**        **Sara Josephine Baker**        **John C. Warren**
    **William Beaumont**        **Jonas Salk**

---

1. "Observing the 'man with the window in his stomach' was remarkable," said _____ in 1833. "I learned that the stomach does not grind or cook food, but instead gastric juices break it down in the digestive process."

2. "In 1955, I introduced a polio vaccine," said _____.

3. "I remember when I used an anesthesia for the first time in surgery," said _____. "When the patient woke up after the operation, he told me he had felt no pain."

4. "I discovered that tuberculosis was not hereditary, but rather was caused by 'tubercle bacillus' and was passed into the air from infected lungs," said _____.

5. "I felt that through proper hygienic training, mothers and nurses could help prevent children from becoming ill," said _____. "Back in 1908, it was difficult convincing city officials to adopt this concept of 'preventive medicine' to keep babies healthy."

Name _____

Date _____

# A Visit to a Shaker Community

**Directions:** Below is an imaginary letter written by a visitor to a Shaker community. Now that you are familiar with the lifestyle and beliefs of a Shaker, you will notice a problem with the letter. Some statements about Shakers are correct, and others are not. Draw a line through those statements about Shakers that are *not* correct.

Dear Ann,

I thought I would write to let you know how much I am enjoying my visit at the Shaker village. It has been a busy spring. Today I worked hard in Mary's garden. She has an especially lovely herb plot. Her husband, Mark, stayed inside to draft a political speech to support his candidate for Congress.

Benjamin has been busy making his slat-back chairs, and he has just completed a fine rocker with arms. You remember Frederick, don't you? Well, he has left to enlist in the military for two years. His cousin, Mark, is still tending the dairy herd. Martha has been her usual self, baking the best pies and breads for the community. By the way, Sara won the lottery and plans to build herself a fine mansion on the hill.

Well, it is time I join the rest of the community for dinner and scripture reading. I do hope this letter finds you well.

Sincerely,

Jane Owens

Name _____

Date _____

# Making a Braille Alphabet

**Directions:** The Braille alphabet is shown below. (Numbers have not been included.) Glue split peas on the dots to complete the raised alphabet. When finished, construct a short Braille sentence at the bottom of the page for others to read.

a    b    c    d    e    f    g

h    i    j    k    l    m    n

o    p    q    r    s    t    u

v    w    x    y    z

\*\*\*\*\*\*\*\*\*\*\*\*\*\*\*\*\*\*\*\*\*\*\*\*

Construct your own short sentence below:

Name _____

Date _____

# Unscrambling a Public Works Message

**Directions:** Unscramble the letters to spell out words that are related to public works. Then unscramble the circled letters to answer the following question: What do you call manmade ducts that supply water to a community or city from a distance?

1. KSTARC   _ _ _Ⓞ_ _

2. IDBERG   _ _ _Ⓞ_ _

3. ESERW   Ⓞ_ _ _ _

4. VUIQRE   Ⓞ_ _ _ _ _

5. DMA   _Ⓞ_

6. YSBAUW   _Ⓞ_ _ _ _

7. ARWET   _ _ _Ⓞ_

8. USB   _Ⓞ_

9. T P S T N O N A R T R I A O
_ _ _ _ _ _ _ _ _ _Ⓞ_ _ _ _

1. What trains travel on.

2. A structure that is built across water or a road to allow passage.

3. An underground drain to carry waste and water.

4. Something you might do if you walked on a suspension bridge.

5. A structure that holds back water.

6. An underground railroad.

7. A natural resource we need to survive.

8. One form of public transportation that moves several people at a time.

9. The business of moving passengers or goods from one place to another.

Put the circled letters here: _ _ _ _ _ _ _ _ _ _

Now unscramble them to answer the above question: _ _ _ _ _ _ _ _ _ _

Name _____

Date _____

# A Jazzy Crossword Puzzle

**Directions:** Test your knowledge of jazz in this puzzle. The clues are below.

Across

1. The last name of a famous jazz trumpet player.

5. A lively, rhythmical form of music.

6. The rhythms of jazz have their roots here.

8. The act of changing and experimenting with music as it is played.

9. The last name of a famous blues singer.

Down

2. The first syllable of this brass wind instrument is its inventor's last name.

3. This city is known as the "cradle of jazz."

4. It is characterized by jerky rhythms in its tunes.

7. He was "King of Ragtime."

Name _____

Date _____

# Finding the Key Word

**Directions:**   Below is a list of questions. Underline the key word you would use to look up the answers in an encyclopedia or a book index.

1.  When was the telegraph invented?

2.  What city is the capital of Utah?

3.  What is the diet of a caribou?

4.  What is the Thirteenth Amendment to the Constitution?

5.  What language is spoken in Brazil?

6.  Was Thomas Jefferson in favor of a strong central government?

7.  What is the climate of Greece?

8.  How many moons orbit the planet of Jupiter?

9.  Which country produces the most wheat in the world?

10.  How does a telephone work?

11.  What type of instrument did Louis Armstrong play?

12.  Where was America's first lighthouse built?

13.  What is the oldest building in America?

14.  When did the Mayflower sail to America?

15.  How did Patrick Henry feel about writing a constitution?

Name _____

Date _____

# How Well Did You Listen?

**Directions:**   This is a listening test. Someone will read the article "Living in the Dust Bowl." The questions and answers below will also be read once to you. Circle the letter of the correct answer.

1. In which decade did the Dust Bowl occur?

    A.   1920s                              C.   1940s

    B.   1930s                              D.   1950s

2. A "black blizzard" was a wall of flying:

    A.   insects                            C.   soil

    B.   mud                                D.   soot

3. Which of these was mentioned as a problem for Great Plains farmers?

    A.   poor fertilizer                    C.   locust plague

    B.   acid soil                          D.   windstorms

4. A native of North Dakota recalled that by noon each day the sky was:

    A.   pale yellow                        C.   grayish

    B.   slightly pink                      D.   black

5. Only one of these was mentioned as a problem homeowners faced. Which was it?

    A.   The houses needed painting.        C.   Dust clogged the chimneys.

    B.   Dust covered everything in the home.   D.   The sidewalks cracked.

6. According to the article, which of these activities continued during the Dust Bowl?

    A.   harvest festivals                  C.   football tournaments

    B.   planting of crops                  D.   fund-raising events

Name _____

Date _____

# First Prize: A Day With Mark Twain

**Directions:** Write a paragraph describing how you would choose to spend a day with Mark Twain.

_____

_____

_____

_____

_____

_____

_____

_____

_____

_____

_____

_____

_____

_____

_____

_____

Name _____

Date _____

# A Bar Graph: Which Program Would Help You?

**Directions:** Students were questioned to see which type of academic computer program would help them in a particular subject. The results are shown in the box. Below the box are questions for you to answer. Then make a bar graph using the information about which computer programs were needed.

| | |
|---|---|
| Spelling | 卌 ||| |
| Math Facts | 卌 卌 || |
| State Capitals | 卌 |
| Word Definitions | ||| |
| Our Solar System | || |

1. How many students wanted a math facts program?  _____

2. How many wanted one on the solar system?  _____

3. How many more wanted state capitals than word definitions?  _____

### Computer Programs Needed by Students

Number of Students Responding

```
16 _____
14 _____
12 _____
10 _____
 8 _____
 6 _____
 4 _____
 2 _____
 0 _____
```

| Spelling | Math Facts | State Capitals | Word Definitions | Solar System |